Old Original
BOOKBINDER'S
Restaurant

COOKBOOK
Judith Frazin

D0064069

Library of Congress Cataloging in Publication Data

Library of Congress Catalog Card Number:
91-093072

International Standard Book No. 0-9631189-0-0

Printed in the United States of America

For my mother,

Lena Wasserman Greene

CONTENTS

INTRODUCTION

The American Civil War was just ending when Samuel and Sarah Bookbinder opened a small restaurant at the dockside of the Delaware River in Philadelphia, cradle of American independence. All the ingredients needed for a great restaurant were literally at their doorstep. Philadelphia was already historically rich and filled with tradition: William Penn's Slate Roof House stood just around the corner; Carpenter's Hall, site of the first Continental Congress, and Independence Hall - home of the Liberty Bell - were minutes away. Nearby were many historical inns such as the Tun Tavern, home of the U.S. Marines; and the shop of the famous gunsmith, Krider, was right next door to the restaurant. Philadelphia was a thriving port city and the Chesapeake was one of the world's great fisheries. Fresh produce arrived daily from the fields surrounding Philadelphia.

It was in this setting that Sarah Bookbinder would ring the bell at noontime announcing the principal meal of the day to dock workers along the Delaware, sea captains and sailors, merchants and farmers, and employees of the Dock Street food market. With its reputation for the choicest produce, meats, and straight from the sea freshness, a new Philadelphia tradition soon began: seafood at Bookbinder's.

The thriving little restaurant passed to the Bookbinder children and stayed in the family until the Depression era when it almost went under. But in 1941, it was taken over by John Taxin, a dynamic man, whose energy, personal magnetism and business savvy, built the enormous success that Old Original Bookbinder's is today.

Bookbinder's is a charming and unique restaurant with several dining rooms, banquet facilities and three bars. One of the bars, imported from a ghost town in Nevada, is one of the longest and most beautiful mahogany bars in existence. The entrance is an old wheelhouse and everywhere you look is all manner of American antiques and memorabilia, such as ships' models, antique cash registers, toys and fire trucks, Currier and Ives prints, old maps and letters, and in the President's Bar is the Pach Collection, portraits of every American president. The fireplace in the Main Dining Room is flanked by Revolutionary War cannons and built with cobblestones worn smooth by the tramping of British and Colonial soldiers. And yes, you can still see Sarah Bookbinder's bell here too. It is no wonder that the restaurant has been designated an historical landmark.

Today, over 125 years since Samuel Bookbinder first opened his doors, the Taxin family members, including son Albert, daughter Sandy, and grandson John E., are keenly aware of the glorious tradition that has been built here and continue to be dedicated to excellence and the same formula that made the restaurant great in Samuel Bookbinder's day: the choicest seafood, and the finest quality meat, fruits and vegetables available.

The great specialty of Bookbinder's has always been fish and shellfish and the recipes in this cookbook reflect this emphasis. However, there is a large selection of other menu items including meats and poultry, soups and chowders, and of course, desserts. Additionally, in an effort to keep pace with America's changing eating habits, new dishes are often tried such as hot and cold pastas, and salads. I have taken some liberties with the restaurant recipes, but no more than necessary to adapt them for home use. I hope I have succeeded in providing a well-rounded representation of all that this venerable dining institution has to offer and that you enjoy much success and many memorable dining moments using your *Old Original Bookbinder's Restaurant Cookbook.*

On a personal note, the preparation of this book has truly been a labor of love, made sweeter by the people who have helped me. I extend thanks to my friends on the west coast who have contributed helpful suggestions and advice; and to my friends at the restaurant: the great kitchen staff and servers, the office staff, and especially the Taxin family, all of whom have offered unlimited encouragement and support, and made me feel that I too, am a part of the tradition that is Old Original Bookbinder's.

And finally, a special thank you to Mark, without whom I'd still be trying to turn on the computer.

Judith Frazin

Appetizers

AVOCADO YOGURT DIP

1 medium avocado
2 tablespoons plain yogurt
dash paprika
1 tablespoon mayonnaise
⅛ teaspoon dry mustard
1 tablespoon hot salsa

Mash avocado and mix in other ingredients. Makes 2 servings.

CHILI CHEESE APPETIZER

½ cup butter or margarine
10 eggs
½ cup flour
1 teaspoon baking powder
dash salt
1 (8-ounce) can chopped green chilies (mild variety)
1 pint cottage cheese
1 pound jack cheese, shredded

Melt butter in 13X9X2 pan. Beat eggs lightly in large bowl. Add flour, baking powder, salt and blend. Add melted butter, chilies, cottage cheese, jack cheese, and mix until blended. Turn batter into pan and bake at 400 degrees for 15 minutes. Reduce heat to 350 degrees and bake 35 to 40 minutes longer. Cut into squares and serve hot. Makes 64 bite-size squares. May be frozen.

6 Appetizers

ACAPULCO DIP

10½-ounce jalapeño bean dip
6¾-ounce avocado dip
½ cup mayonnaise and ½ cup sour cream,
  mixed together
1 packet taco seasoning
1½ cups shredded cheddar cheese
1½ cups shredded jack cheese
1 cup chopped green onions
2 tomatoes, chopped
1 can black olives, sliced

Layer in this order in serving dish. Cover and
refrigerate until ready to serve.

HERRING APPETIZER

1 (12-ounce) jar pickled herring, drained and cut up
1 diced green pepper
2 small cans black olives, sliced
1 small jar pickled artichoke hearts, cut up
¼ cup chopped parsley
1 (12-ounce) bottle chili sauce

Combine all ingredients and refrigerate until ready to use.

CLAMS CASINO

12 cherrystone clams on the halfshell
4 tablespoons finely chopped green pepper
4 tablespoons finely chopped pimiento
2 strips bacon, cut in small pieces
2 tablespoons melted butter
paprika

Place clams in a tin plate, half filled with rock salt (use enough rock salt to hold the shellfish firmly in place). Sprinkle each with bits of green pepper and pimiento. Place pieces of bacon on top. Sprinkle with melted butter and a dash of paprika. Bake in a hot oven, 400 degrees, for 10 minutes. Turn bacon once so that it will crisp on both sides. Serves 2.

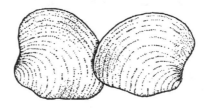

SHRIMP COCKTAIL*

10-12 large cooked shrimp
6 tablespoons cocktail or Lamaze Sauce, see page 70
lemon wedges

Put one tablespoon of sauce in the bottom of each cocktail glass. Place three shrimp on top. Add another tablespoon of sauce, the rest of the shrimp and a third tablespoon of sauce. Serve with a wedge of lemon on the side. Makes 1 serving.

*For lobster or crabmeat cocktail, make the same way, substituting ½ cup seafood for shrimp.

SHRIMP MOUSSE

1 can tomato soup
1 (8-ounce) package cream cheese
1½ cups chopped celery
1½ cups chopped onion
3 small cans shrimp, mashed
1 cup mayonnaise
1½ envelopes gelatin
1 teaspoon dill weed

Melt soup and cheese together with gelatin. Add remaining ingredients; put in oiled mold and refrigerate.

SHRIMP WITH ARTICHOKES

1 pound cooked shrimp
¾ cup sour cream
¾ cup mayonnaise
1 tablespoon Worcestershire sauce
dash Tabasco
1½ tablespoons chili sauce
1 purple onion, thinly sliced
1 large can drained artichoke hearts, cut in half

Combine sour cream, mayonnaise, Worcestershire sauce, Tabasco, and chili sauce. Add shrimp, onion, and artichoke. Refrigerate until ready to use. Serves 6.

SOFTSHELL CRABS SAUTÉ

12 small soft shell crabs
salt and pepper
flour
¼ cup butter or margarine
¼ cup vegetable oil
lemon juice

Clean crabs thoroughly. Season the crabs with salt and pepper and dip them into flour. Heat butter and oil together and sauté crabs in the mixture until golden brown. To serve, pour the juices from the pan over the crabs and add a squeeze of lemon juice. Serves 4.

CRAB BALLS

1 tablespoon chopped green pepper
1 tablespoon minced onion
1 tablespoon minced celery
1 tablespoon minced pimiento
salt and pepper
½ teaspoon thyme
1 teaspoon Worcestershire sauce
2 tablespoons butter or margarine
4 tablespoons flour
1 cup milk
1 pound crabmeat
Egg Batter, see page 71
bread crumbs
cooking oil

Mix vegetables and seasonings together and cook in the butter over low heat for 10 minutes, taking care not to brown the vegetables. Add flour and stir to blend well. Cook, stirring, for 5 minutes. Add milk and stir until thickened. Add crabmeat and mix well. Chill the mixture thoroughly. Form into bite-size balls, dip into *Egg Batter*, then into crumbs and fry in oil, 375 degrees, until nicely browned. Makes 15-20 balls.

THYME

OYSTERS ROCKEFELLER

12 oysters on the halfshell
rock salt
2 teaspoons butter
2 teaspoons finely minced onion
2 teaspoons finely minced celery
flour
4 tablespoons spinach, cooked and chopped
salt and pepper
nutmeg, fresh if possible
½ teaspoon Worcestershire sauce
2 tablespoons Parmesan cheese
2 tablespoons bread crumbs
butter

Melt butter in pan. Sauté onion and celery in it until soft, but not brown. Dredge lightly with flour. Season spinach to taste with salt and pepper. Give it a good grind of fresh nutmeg and add Worcestershire sauce. Place oysters on a bed of rock salt (enough to hold them firmly in place) in a pie plate. Place in a 375 degree oven, to heat for 3-4 minutes. Mix onion and celery with spinach mixture. Remove oysters from the oven and cover each with spinach mixture. Mix the cheese and bread crumbs and sprinkle over the oysters. Dot each lightly with butter. Return oysters to the oven and bake 10-12 minutes, or until brown. Serves 2.

SMOKED OYSTER ROLL

1 medium clove garlic, crushed
1 medium shallot
2 (8-ounce) packages cream cheese, room temperature
2 tablespoons mayonnaise
2 tablespoons Worcestershire sauce
¼ teaspoon salt
⅛ teaspoon white pepper
dash Tabasco
2 (3¾-ounce) cans smoked oysters, drained
½ cup finely chopped walnuts
crackers or bread rounds

In a food processor with metal blade, mix garlic, shallot, cream cheese, mayonnaise, Worcestershire sauce, salt, pepper, and Tabasco until blended. Spread mixture on piece of aluminum foil into a rectangle approximately 8"X10".

In same bowl, mash oysters. Spread over cream cheese. Cover loosely with plastic wrap and refrigerate 5 hours or more until firm. Use a long narrow spatula to release cream cheese from foil. Roll like a jelly roll and shape into log. Roll in nuts and cover completely. May refrigerate in wrap for 3 days. Garnish with pimiento and parsley. Serves 8-10.

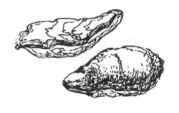

Soups

BOUILLABAISSE

½ pound shrimp
½ pound codfish
½ pound scallops
6 oysters
2 tablespoons minced onion
1 clove garlic, minced
2 tablespoons minced celery
2 tablespoons minced green pepper
½ cup butter
½ cup flour
2 cups stock from fish
1 cup cooked lobster meat

Shell and clean the shrimp, saving the shells. Tie the codfish in cheesecloth. Place the codfish, scallops, shrimp, and oysters in salted water to cover. Bring to boiling, then reduce heat and simmer 5 minutes. Drain, reserving stock. Place shrimp shells in stock and cook it until it is reduced to 4 cups. Strain through a cheesecloth. Meantime, cook onion, garlic, celery, and green pepper in butter until soft, but not brown. Add flour and stir thoroughly until smooth. Add 2 cups stock and stir until thickened. Dice the codfish, lobster, scallops, and shrimp. Add to thickened soup and heat through. There will be 2 cups of fish stock left for future use; store this in a covered container in the refrigerator or freezer. Serves 6.

FISH STOCK

3 pounds bones from a white-fleshed, nonoily fish,
  including heads if possible, but with gills removed
8 cups water
1 cup dry white wine
1 cup coarsely chopped celery
1 cup coarsely chopped carrots
1 cup coarsely chopped onions
4 sprigs fresh parsley
3 sprigs fresh thyme or 1 teaspoon dried
1 bay leaf
10 peppercorns
salt to taste
1 medium-size tomato, cored, optional

Run the bones under cold running water. Place the bones
in a large deep saucepan and add the remaining
ingredients. Bring to a boil and simmer for 20 minutes.
Strain and discard the solids. Makes 10 cups and may be
frozen.

FISH SOUP WITH TOMATOES

3 tablespoons olive oil
4 teaspoons finely minced garlic
2 cups finely chopped onions
2 cups finely diced, trimmed leeks, green part and all
1 cup finely chopped celery
1 teaspoon (2 grams) loosely packed thread saffron
⅛ teaspoon dried hot red-pepper flakes
¼ teaspoon ground turmeric
3 cups crushed tomatoes
¼ teaspoon dried fennel seeds
1 bay leaf
2 sprigs fresh thyme
salt to taste, if desired
freshly ground pepper to taste
1 cup dry white wine
6 cups *Fish Stock*, see page 17
2 small squid, about ¾ pound, thoroughly cleaned
1½ pounds skinless, boneless blackfish, red snapper,
   or other white-fleshed, nonoily fish
18 littleneck clams
1 quart mussels
2 tablespoons anise-flavored liqueur such as
   Pernod
½ cup finely chopped parsley

Heat the oil in a deep pot with a heavy bottom and add the garlic and onions. Cook, stirring, until the onions are wilted. Add the leeks, celery, saffron, red-pepper flakes and turmeric. Cook, stirring, about 5 minutes without browning.

Add the tomatoes, fennel seeds, bay leaf, thyme, salt and pepper. Add the wine and bring to the boil. Let simmer five minutes. Add the stock and continue cooking 10 minutes.

Meanwhile, cut the bodies of the squid into rings; cut the tentacles into small pieces and set aside. There should be about one cup. Cut the fish into 1-inch cubes and set aside. There should be about three cups. Thoroughly rinse the clams and drain. Set aside.

When the soup mixture has cooked 10 minutes after the stock has been added, add the clams. Stir and let cook five minutes. Add the mussels and cook one minute. Add the fish, squid, Pernod and parsley and cook 1-2 minutes. Do not overcook or the fish will become dry. Remove the bay leaf and serve immediately. Makes about 10 servings.

HEARTY FISH CHOWDER

6 tablespoons butter or margarine
1 cup chopped onion
1 large leek, chopped
3 stalks celery, cut into 1½x¼-inch sticks
2 large carrots, cut into 1½x¼-inch sticks
¼ pound mushrooms, sliced
¼ cup flour
½ teaspoon thyme
½ teaspoon salt
⅛ teaspoon black pepper
2½ cups milk
1 (10¾-ounce) can condensed chicken broth
½ cup whipping cream
2 large bay leaves
1 pound white fish, cut into 1-inch pieces
1 cup diced cooked potatoes

Melt butter in 4-quart Dutch oven. Add onion, leek, celery and carrots and cook until tender, about 10 minutes. Add mushrooms and cook 2 minutes longer. Remove from heat. Stir in flour, thyme, salt and pepper until smooth. Gradually stir in milk, broth and cream. Bring to a boil, stirring constantly. Boil and stir 1 minute. Add fish. Cover and simmer until fish flakes easily with fork, about 10 minutes. Stir in potatoes. Heat to serving temperature. Makes 9 cups.

LOBSTER BISQUE

1 tablespoon finely minced celery
1 tablespoon finely minced onion
3 tablespoons butter
¼ cup flour
4 cups lobster stock
¼ cup cream
salt and white pepper
dash freshly ground nutmeg
1 cup diced lobster meat

Sauté celery and onion in butter until soft, but not brown. Sprinkle with the flour and mix well. Add lobster stock and cream and stir until thickened. Season to taste with salt, pepper, and nutmeg. Add lobster meat and heat through. Serves 4.

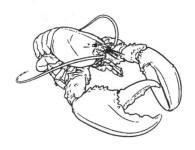

MANHATTAN CLAM CHOWDER

2 cups large clams, cooked
2 medium sliced onions
2 large potatoes, diced
2 bell peppers, finely chopped
2 stalks of celery, finely chopped
2 tablespoons butter or margarine
1 tablespoon paprika
2 tablespoons of clam base
1 quart clam stock
1 (12-ounce) can whole tomatoes
2 tablespoons flour
1 tablespoon all-purpose seasoning,
   such as *Accent*

Steam clams and reserve liquid to use as clam stock. Dice cooked clams. Cook potatoes separately in boiling water.

In large pot, sauté onions, peppers, celery, and paprika in butter until the vegetables are tender. Add flour and *Accent*, stirring well so that mixture does not brown. Add clam stock and clam base. Add potatoes and clams. Allow to simmer for fifteen minutes. Add chopped and drained tomatoes and simmer for five to ten minutes, covered.

ONION SOUP WITH FISH

4 tablespoons butter
2 teaspoons finely minced garlic
8 cups coarsely chopped onions, about 2½ pounds
¼ cup flour
1 cup dry white wine
8 cups *Fish Stock*, see page 17
1 bay leaf
1 or 2 dried hot red peppers
salt to taste, if desired
freshly ground pepper to taste
2 pounds skinless, boneless blackfish, red snapper,
    or other white-fleshed, nonoily fish

Heat the butter in a deep pot with a heavy bottom and
add the garlic. Cook briefly without browning. Add the
onions and cook, stirring, until they are golden brown,
about 15 minutes. Do not burn. Sprinkle with the flour
and stir to blend well.

Add the wine, stirring, and bring to a boil. Add the fish
stock, bay leaf, dried red peppers, salt and pepper. Bring
to a boil and let simmer, uncovered, about 15 minutes.
Cut the fish into 1-inch cubes. There should be about
four cups. After the broth mixture has cooked 15
minutes, add the cubed fish and let cook about four
minutes. Do not overcook or the fish will become dry.
Scoop out and discard the hot peppers and bay leaf.
Makes 6 to 8 servings.

SHRIMP, CRAB, AND SEAFOOD GUMBO

2 tablespoons butter
4 tablespoons flour
1 medium onion, chopped
4 tomatoes, chopped
3 quarts soup stock or water
1 quart okra, sliced thin
1 pound raw shrimp, shelled
1 pound raw crabmeat
20 oysters, shucked
salt and pepper
chopped parsley

Melt the butter in a deep saucepan, add the flour, and blend. Add the chopped onion, and cook over medium heat until it is browned. Stir in the tomatoes, the soup stock, and the okra. Cut the shrimp and crabmeat into bite-size pieces, add to the stock, and simmer them all together until the okra is tender. Add the oysters and the seasonings, and heat over a low flame until the oysters have become plump. Sprinkle each serving with chopped parsley and serve at once.

PEPPER POT SOUP

1 pound honeycomb tripe
6 cups beef stock
1 medium green pepper, diced
¼ cup diced celery
¼ cup diced onion
1 cup stewed tomatoes
1 cup diced uncooked potatoes
  or 1 cup shell pasta
¼ teaspoon thyme
1 small clove garlic, mashed
dash Tabasco
salt and pepper
¼ cup bacon fat
¼ cup flour

Cook the tripe in one piece in the stock about 3 hours, or until tender. Drain, reserving stock. Cool, chill, and cut into strips. If there are not 4 cups of tripe stock, add enough beef stock to make it 4 cups. Add green pepper, celery, onion, tomatoes, and potatoes or pasta, together with the seasonings, and cook until vegetables are done (about 20 minutes). Melt the bacon fat and add flour, stirring until smooth. Add stock and vegetables and stir until thickened. Add tripe and heat through. Correct seasoning. Serves 4 to 6.

SNAPPER SOUP*

3½ pounds veal knuckle, broken into 2-inch pieces
1 cup chicken fat or butter
3 onions, chopped fine
2 stalks celery, chopped
2 carrots, diced
½ teaspoon thyme
½ teaspoon marjoram
3 whole cloves
1 bay leaf
salt and pepper
1 cup flour
4 quarts beef broth
2 cups strained tomatoes
meat from 1 snapper turtle, cut in small pieces
2 cups dry sherry
dash Tabasco sauce
3 slices lemon
1 hard-cooked egg, chopped

Place knuckles in a roasting pan and add the butter or chicken fat, onions, celery, carrots, thyme, marjoram, cloves, bay leaf, and salt and pepper to taste. Bake in a 400 degree oven until brown (about 30 minutes). Remove from oven and add flour, mixing well. Reduce oven heat to 350 degrees and cook 30 minutes longer. Pour mixture into a large soup kettle. Add broth and tomatoes. Simmer for 3½ hours. Combine the snapper meat with 1 cup sherry, a dash of salt, Tabasco, and the lemon slices. Simmer for 10 minutes. Strain the soup and combine with the snapper mixture. Add chopped egg and the remaining 1 cup dry sherry. Heat through and serve at once. This makes over a gallon.

*If you cannot find snapper turtle, you may order the soup in cans from *Bookbinder's Gift Shop.*

TOMATO BISQUE

2 pounds ripe tomatoes, diced
2 medium onions, diced
½ cup diced celery
1 carrot, diced
turkey or chicken carcass
chicken stock to cover (4 to 6 cups)
salt and pepper
dash of fresh ground nutmeg
2 cups cream or half-and-half

Place vegetables, carcass of fowl, and stock in kettle. Bring to the boil and simmer, covered, 1 hour. Remove fowl carcass and whirl soup in the blender or press through a sieve. Season to taste with salt, pepper, and nutmeg. Thicken, if desired, with butter and flour until smoothly blended. Add cream and heat through. Serves 6 to 8.

MINESTRONE SOUP

4 tablespoons butter
1 large onion, minced
1 large carrot, diced
2 stalks celery
½ green pepper, diced
2 medium zucchini, diced
1 cup spinach, shredded
1 cup savoy cabbage, shredded
3 cans chicken broth
1 can water
1 cup cannellini beans
½ cup small pasta
1 cup canned tomatoes
juice of tomatoes
2 cloves garlic
2 teaspoons oregano
optional: string beans, potatoes

Sauté onion in butter for 10 minutes. Add carrot, celery, green pepper and green beans. Stew to bring out flavor. Add chicken broth, water and all vegetables. Simmer until all other vegetables are crisp tender. Purée juice of tomatoes, garlic and oregano. Add tomatoes and purée and check seasonings. Soup is better if prepared a day ahead. Serves 6-8

SPINACH CRAB SOUP

1 can (7½-ounce) crab meat
1 (10-ounce) package frozen leaf spinach
3 tablespoons butter or margarine
1 cup diced celery
½ cup chopped onions
2 tablespoons flour
½ teaspoon salt
⅛ teaspoon black pepper
⅛ teaspoon nutmeg
2 cups chicken broth
2 cups half-and-half

Drain and slice crab, reserving liquid. Cook spinach according to package directions. Drain and chop coarsely. Melt butter in large saucepan. Add celery and onions and sauté until tender. Blend in flour, salt, pepper and nutmeg. Gradually add broth, stirring constantly. Heat to boiling. Add half-and-half and reserved crab liquid. Stir in crab and spinach. Cook until heated through. Makes 4-6 servings.

CHILLED ZUCCHINI SOUP

⅓ cup butter or margarine
1 cup sliced green onions
1 clove garlic, minced
3 cups sliced zucchini
1 cup water
2 chicken bouillon cubes
½ teaspoon salt
¼ teaspoon pepper
4 cups milk
2 tablespoons cornstarch
¼ cup sauterne or dry vermouth
2 teaspoons dill weed, chopped
½ cup finely diced raw zucchini
packaged croutons, optional

In large saucepan, melt butter over medium heat. Add onion and garlic. Cook 5 minutes or until tender. Add zucchini slices. Cook and stir 10 minutes or until zucchini is very soft. Add water, bouillon cubes, salt and pepper. Cover and simmer 15 minutes. Place in blender, a little at a time. Cover and blend 30 seconds or until liquefied. Return to saucepan.

Stir milk into cornstarch. Add to soup. Cook and stir over medium heat until soup boils for 1 minute. Stir in sauterne and dill. Cover and chill several hours or overnight. Before serving, add more dill if needed, garnish with diced zucchini and croutons. Makes 1½ quarts.

CHILLED SPINACH SOUP

¼ cup butter or margarine
¼ cup diced onion
¼ cup flour
1 teaspoon salt
½ teaspoon dry mustard
¼ teaspoon nutmeg
1 (10¾-ounce) can condensed chicken broth
1 (10-ounce) package frozen chopped spinach
½ cup shredded carrot
2½ cups milk

Melt butter in 2-quart saucepan. Add onion and cook until tender. Blend in flour, salt, mustard and nutmeg. Remove from heat and stir in chicken broth. Bring to boil, stirring constantly. Add spinach and carrot and cook over medium heat, stirring occasionally, until carrot is tender and spinach thawed. Cool. Purée in blender. Stir in milk. Cover and chill. Can garnish with lemon slices if desired. Makes 6 servings.

COLD BROCCOLI SOUP

1 ½ pounds broccoli, trimmed
4 cups chicken broth
1 cup yogurt
⅛ to ¼ teaspoon all-spice
¼ teaspoon crushed dried basil
salt to taste
¼ teaspoon white pepper to taste
thin lemon slices for garnish

Cook broccoli until tender in boiling broth. Cool in broth.
Finely chop broccoli in blender. Add cooking liquid as
needed for blending. Combine yogurt with broccoli,
remaining broth, spice and basil. Season to taste with
salt and pepper. Cover and chill until ready to serve.
Garnish with lemon slices. Makes 6 servings.

GAZPACHO

2 large tomatoes (1¾ pounds), peeled
1 large cucumber, pared and halved
1 medium onion, peeled and halved
1 medium green pepper, cut in half and seeded
2 cloves garlic
1 pimiento, drained
2 cans (12-ounce size) tomato juice
¼ cup olive or salad oil
⅓ cup red-wine vinegar
⅛ teaspoon Tabasco sauce
1½ teaspoons salt, optional
dash coarsely ground black pepper
2 cloves garlic, split
½ cup packaged croutons
¼ cup chopped chives

In food processor or electric blender, combine one tomato, half the cucumber, half the onion, half the green pepper, the pimiento, garlic, and ½ cup of tomato juice. Blend covered at high speed to purée the vegetables. Pour into large bowl.

Chop remaining tomato, ½ cucumber, ½ onion, and ½ green pepper. Add to purée, along with remaining tomato juice, oil, vinegar, Tabasco, salt and pepper. Refrigerate mixture, covered, until it is well chilled - at least 2 hours. Serve with packaged croutons and chives and sour cream if desired. Serves 6.

CUCUMBER SOUP

3 cucumbers, peeled and sliced
2 tablespoons butter or margarine
1 leek, sliced without the green
1 bay leaf
1 tablespoon flour
3 cups chicken broth
1 teaspoon salt
1 cup whipping cream or half-and-half
juice of ½ lemon
1 teaspoon fresh dill, finely chopped
salt and pepper

Sauté 2 cucumbers in butter with leek and bay leaf for 20 minutes or until tender but not browned. Stir in flour. Add chicken broth and salt and simmer 30 minutes. Put mixture in blender half at a time, then strain through a sieve. Chill.

Add the remaining cucumber, which has been peeled and grated, the cream and lemon juice. Stir in dill and correct seasoning with salt and pepper. Chill until very cold. Serves 6.

DILL

WATERCRESS CUCUMBER SOUP

2 large potatoes, diced, (about 3 cups)
6 medium leeks (tops removed), chopped
2 (12-ounce) cans beer
3 cups chicken stock
1 tablespoon salt
2 bunches watercress
2 medium cucumbers, peeled and sliced
¾ cup whipping cream or half-and-half

Place potatoes, leeks, beer, chicken stock and salt in large saucepan. Bring to a boil. Reduce heat, cover and add watercress leaves to soup. Cook 5 minutes more. Remove from heat and stir in cucumber slices. Cool. Purée in blender until smooth.

Stir in cream and chill well. Garnish with more watercress and cucumber slices if desired. Makes about 2½ quarts.

Salads

CAESAR SALAD

1 clove garlic
¾ cup salad oil
2 cups white bread cubes (prepared croutons
  may be used)
2 eggs
3 tablespoons fresh lemon juice
2 teaspoons Worcestershire sauce
½ teaspoon salt or to taste
¼ teaspoon pepper
8 anchovy fillets, chopped
2 heads romaine lettuce, washed and chilled
¼ cup crumbled blue cheese
¼ cup grated Parmesan cheese

Crush garlic and cover with oil in a bowl for at least 30 minutes. Measure ¼ cup garlic oil in frying pan and fry bread cubes until brown on all sides. Set aside.

In a small bowl, combine the lemon juice, Worcestershire, salt, pepper, and anchovies; mix well.

In a large bowl, tear lettuce into bite-size pieces. Drain remaining oil from garlic. Pour over lettuce; toss to coat evenly. Break eggs over lettuce and toss well. Pour on lemon mixture, toss again, and add bread cubes and cheeses. Toss well and serve immediately. Serves 8-10.

CHOPPED SALAD

2 cups romaine lettuce
2 cups butter lettuce
2 cups red leaf lettuce
2 cups snow peas
2 cups radishes
2 cups carrots
1 zucchini
1 red bell pepper
1 cup mushrooms
dressing, such as a creamy Italian
freshly ground pepper

Dice all vegetables very fine. Add pepper to taste and toss well with dressing. Serves 6-8.

COBB SALAD

½ head iceberg lettuce
½ bunch watercress
1 small bunch curly endive
½ head romaine
2 tablespoons minced chives
2 medium tomatoes, peeled, seeded and diced
1 whole chicken breast, cooked, boned,
  skinned and diced
6 strips bacon, cooked and diced
1 avocado, peeled and diced
3 hard-cooked eggs, diced
½ cup Roquefort cheese, crumbled, optional
French Dressing, see page 68

Chop lettuce, watercress, endive and romaine into very fine pieces using knife or food processor. Mix together in a large wide bowl. Add chives; arrange tomatoes, chicken, bacon, avocado and eggs across top of greens. Sprinkle with cheese, chill. At serving time, toss with ½ cup *French Dressing* or any other dressing. Pass remaining dressing. Makes 6 servings.

SHRIMP SALAD

1 cup cooked shrimp*
2 hard cooked eggs, chopped
½ cup grated raw carrots
1 tablespoon minced onion
½ teaspoon salt
⅛ teaspoon pepper
½ cup mayonnaise
2 tablespoons lemon juice
½ teaspoon prepared mustard
3-4 large tomatoes, sliced
salad greens

Combine shrimp with eggs, carrots, onion, salt and pepper. Blend mayonnaise with lemon juice and mustard; toss with shrimp mixture. Arrange tomato slices on crisp greens; heap with shrimp and dressing.

This shrimp mixture can also be used as stuffing for tomatoes.

*Other seafood may be added to or substituted for the shrimp.

SPINACH, BACON
AND MUSHROOM SALAD

6 slices bacon
5 cups spinach leaves, washed and torn
2 cups mushrooms, sliced
2 cups endive, slivered
½ cup red onion, thinly sliced
1 cup oranges, thinly sliced
Orange Buttermilk Dressing, see page 68

Fry bacon in skillet until browned and crisp. Drain on
paper towels and crumble. In large bowl, combine
spinach, mushrooms, endive and onion. Drizzle with
dressing and toss gently. Just before serving, add
oranges and bacon and toss again. Makes 4 servings.

CUCUMBER SALAD

2 large cucumbers, peeled and scored
1 medium onion
½ cup vinegar
2 tablespoons sugar
¼ cup water

Slice cucumbers into ice water; drain and pat dry. Peel onion, slice thinly, and add to cucumber slices. Pour vinegar, sugar, and water over the slices, adding more water if necessary. Refrigerate several hours or preferably overnight. Serves 4.

SEAFOOD SALAD

2 tomatoes, cut up
½ cup pine nuts, toasted
½ bunch red lettuce, torn into pieces
½ bunch butter lettuce, torn into pieces
½ bunch romaine lettuce, torn into pieces
radicchio, optional
asparagus, 2-3 stalks per person, optional
1-1½ pounds cooked seafood, such as shrimp,
  crab, scallops, or lobster
Honey Mustard Dressing, see page 69

Combine all ingredients and toss with salad dressing to taste. Makes 6 servings.

*Chicken can be substituted for seafood.

ARTICHOKE PASTA SALAD

10-12 ounces pasta, such as rotelle or macaroni
1 jar (6-ounces) marinated artichoke hearts
¼ pound whole small mushrooms
2 medium-size tomatoes, seeded and cut into
  bite-size pieces
1 cup black olives, pitted and sliced
salt and pepper

Following package directions, cook pasta until al dente.
Drain and rinse with cold water. Turn into a large bowl.

Combine artichokes with the liquid, mushrooms,
tomatoes, and olives. Add mixture to cooked pasta and
toss gently. Cover and refrigerate for several hours or
overnight. Before serving, season to taste with salt and
pepper and if needed, Italian dressing can be added.
Serves 4.

CHICKEN PASTA SALAD

6-ounces rotelle or other pasta twists
¼ cup sesame seeds
½ cup salad oil
⅓ cup soy sauce
⅓ cup white wine vinegar
3 tablespoons sugar
½ teaspoon salt
¼ teaspoon pepper
3 cups cold shredded cooked chicken
½ cup chopped parsley
½ cup green onion, thinly sliced, including tops
8 cups lightly packed torn spinach leaves

Follow package directions and cook pasta until al dente. Drain and rinse in cold water. Turn into a large bowl.

In a small frying pan, combine sesame seeds and ¼ cup of the oil; cook over medium low heat, stirring occasionally, until seeds are golden (about 2 minutes). Let cool. Stir in remaining oil, soy sauce, vinegar, sugar, salt and pepper. Pour over cooked pasta. Add chicken, and toss gently. Cover and chill for at least 2 hours or overnight. To serve, add parsley, onion, and spinach and toss lightly. Serves 3-4.

CHICKEN TARRAGON PASTA SALAD

¼ pound China peas (edible pea pods)
salt
¾ pound rigatoni, penne, or other pasta
⅔-¾ pound cooked chicken, slivered
2 tablespoons chopped tarragon
¼ cup chopped green onions
½ cup mayonnaise
2 teaspoons lemon juice
freshly ground pepper
1 large tomato, chopped

Remove ends and strings from pea pods. Cook in large pot of boiling water with ½ tablespoon salt 1-2 minutes until color turns bright green. Remove pea pods with slotted spoon and rinse under cold water. Spread on towel to cool.

Add rigatoni to same pot of boiling water and cook about 8 minutes or until tender but still firm. Drain, then rinse thoroughly under cold water. Drain again, then place in large bowl.

Slice pea pods into diagonal strips. Add pea pods, chicken, tarragon, and onions to rigatoni. Toss to combine. In small bowl combine mayonnaise and lemon juice. Add to salad and toss. Season to taste with salt and pepper. Serve garnished with chopped tomato.

This can be served cold; if not served immediately, reserve some of mayonnaise mixture and toss in before serving as pasta will absorb dressing as it sits.

CRAB AND ARTICHOKE PASTA SALAD

3-ounces pasta, such as bows
1 ½ tablespoons butter or margarine
1 ½ tablespoons flour
½ cup milk
¼ cup dry white wine or chicken broth
¼ cup Swiss cheese, shredded
1 teaspoon Worcestershire sauce
1 package (9-ounce) frozen artichoke hearts,
  cooked and drained
⅓ pound cooked fresh or canned crab
1 tablespoon grated Parmesan cheese

Cook pasta according to package directions. Meanwhile, melt butter in a small pan over medium heat. Blend in flour and cook, stirring, until bubbly. Remove pan from heat and gradually stir in milk. Return to heat and cook, stirring constantly, until smooth and thickened. Slowly blend in wine, Swiss cheese, and Worcestershire sauce; cook just until cheese melts.

Spoon a thin layer of sauce into a 1 ½ quart casserole. Arrange half the artichokes, crab, and pasta in even layers over the sauce. Cover with half the sauce. Repeat the layering ending with the sauce. Sprinkle with Parmesan cheese and bake in a 350 degree oven for 30 to 35 minutes. Serves 2-3.

CURRIED SALMON SALAD

12-ounces conchiglie or other small shell pasta
½ cup salted shelled sunflower seeds
½ cup finely chopped green pepper
½ cup sliced green onions, including tops
1 cup chopped celery
1 package (10-ounce) frozen peas, thawed and drained
2 cups cooked salmon or 2 cans (7-ounce size) salmon
parsley sprigs
3 hard-cooked eggs, thinly sliced
Curry Dressing, see page 69

Prepare curry dressing and set aside. Follow package
directions and cook pasta until al dente. Drain, rinse with
cold water and rinse again. Turn into large bowl. Add
sunflower seeds, green pepper, onions, celery, and peas.
Add dressing, reserving about ½ cup, and toss. Cover
and chill.

To serve, add remaining dressing if necessary and
spoon pasta salad onto serving platter. Flake salmon onto
the pasta and garnish with parsley and egg slices. Serves
6 to 8.

MARCO POLO PASTA SALAD

½ pound scallops
2 cups lemon juice
½ pound broccoli spears
8-ounces fusilli (corkscrew), tomato-based
1 cup plus 1 tablespoon virgin olive oil
1 cup Greek-style olives
1 tablespoon capers, chopped
2 tablespoons soy sauce
salt, pepper
julienned pimiento

Marinate scallops in lemon juice overnight. Drain and discard juice. Parboil broccoli in 1-inch boiling water until it is crisp but tender and bright green in color, about 4 minutes. Cut into flowerets and julienne stems. Set aside.

Cook pasta in boiling, generously salted water and 1 tablespoon oil until cooked but still firm, about 20 minutes. Drain and rinse in cold water. Turn into large serving bowl. Add scallops, broccoli, olives, capers, 1 cup olive oil, soy sauce and season to taste with salt and pepper. Garnish with pimiento strips. Makes 3-4 servings.

Vegetables

ASPARAGUS WITH DAFFODIL SAUCE

2 egg yolks
2 tablespoons lemon juice
¼ cup half-and-half
1 teaspoon dry mustard
¼ teaspoon salt
½ teaspoon Worcestershire sauce
1 (8-ounce) package cream cheese, cubed
2 teaspoons chopped chives
2 pounds asparagus, cooked and drained

Combine egg yolks, lemon juice, half-and-half, mustard, salt, Worcestershire and cream cheese in blender container and blend at high speed until smooth. Turn into small saucepan and cook and stir over low heat for 5 minutes. Add chopped chives. Serve warm over cooked asparagus. Makes 8 servings.

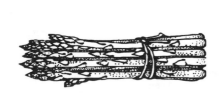

CHIVES

CARROT PUDDING

¼ pound butter or margarine
½ cup brown sugar
2 eggs
1½ cups grated or ground carrots
1 cup sifted flour
1 teaspoon baking powder
½ teaspoon baking soda
pinch salt
1 tablespoon water
1 tablespoon lemon juice

Beat butter and brown sugar together. Add other ingredients. Mix and pour into well greased mold. Bake in 350 degree oven for 30 minutes.

BROCCOLI QUICHE

½ pound mushrooms, sliced
1 package frozen chopped broccoli or 1 pound fresh
2 eggs, beaten
½ cup milk
½ cup mayonnaise
8-ounces jack cheese, shredded
frozen pie shell
margarine or butter

Allow pie shell to defrost while preparing quiche. Sauté mushrooms and onions in margarine or butter. Cook broccoli according to package directions and drain well. If using fresh broccoli, steam until just tender and then immediately immerse in cold water.

Combine all ingredients in large bowl and stir until well blended. Pour into pie shell and bake in preheated 350 degree oven for 45 minutes. Serves 6.

CAULIFLOWER WITH CHEESE
AND GARLIC*

1 medium cauliflower, broken in flowerets
4-6 tablespoons butter or margarine
½ teaspoon pepper
1 teaspoon dill weed
2 cloves garlic, minced, or ½ teaspoon garlic powder
4 tablespoons Parmesan cheese

Melt 4 tablespoons butter and add salt, pepper, dill weed, garlic, and 2 tablespoons Parmesan cheese. Put cauliflower in ovenproof baking dish. Pour sauce over cauliflower and top with 2 tablespoons Parmesan cheese. Put under broiler until brown.

*Note: This sauce can be prepared for Shrimp Scampi.

DILL

LYONNAISE POTATOES

3-6 small red skinned potatoes, cooked
3 tablespoons butter or margarine
1 tablespoon salad oil
⅔ cup coarsely chopped onion
¼ teaspoon salt, optional
⅛ teaspoon freshly ground pepper

Cut the cooked potatoes (cold or hot) into ¼-inch slices. Do not peel. Heat the butter and oil in a large frying pan over medium-high heat. Add the onions, potatoes, salt, and pepper, and sauté until the potatoes are lightly browned and the onions are cooked. Salt and pepper to taste. Makes 3-4 servings.

O'BRIEN POTATOES

2 cups diced cooked potatoes
2 tablespoons diced green pepper
2 pimientos, diced
2 tablespoons butter
2 tablespoons vegetable oil

Mix potatoes, green pepper, and pimiento. Melt butter with oil in a skillet. Add potato mixture and press down firmly. Cover and cook over low heat until golden brown. Turn upside down to serve. Serves 4.

HASHED BROWN POTATOES

2 cups cubed cooked potatoes
salt and pepper
2 tablespoons butter
2 tablespoons vegetable oil
paprika

Season the potato cubes with salt and pepper. Melt butter with oil in a skillet. Add potatoes and press them down firmly. Cover and cook over low heat until golden brown (20 to 30 minutes). Sprinkle with paprika and turn carefully with a spatula to brown the other side.

ITALIAN ZUCCHINI WITH MEAT

3 tablespoons oil
1 medium onion, thinly sliced
1 pound ground sirloin
3 (8-ounce) cans tomato sauce
1 cup red wine
1 teaspoon mixed Italian seasonings
dash garlic powder
1 tablespoon sugar
½ teaspoon salt and pepper
2 pounds zucchini (6-7), washed, trimmed, and sliced
grated Parmesan cheese

Brown meat and onion in oil. Add remaining ingredients except for zucchini. Simmer for 1 hour. Put zucchini in baking dish. Pour sauce over and bake for 45 minutes. Garnish with Parmesan cheese. Serves 4-6.

SAUTÉED ZUCCHINI

2 medium zucchini, cut into ½-inch slices
2 tablespoons butter
1 small onion, sliced
1 teaspoon powdered chicken stock
salt and pepper

Melt the butter in a skillet. Add zucchini, onion and powdered stock, and sauté until the zucchini is soft but not brown (about 10 minutes). If necessary, add more butter. Season to taste with salt and pepper. Serves 4.

ZUCCHINI CASSEROLE

4-6 zucchinis
1 onion, cut up
salt
⅛ pound grated cheddar cheese
¼ teaspoon caraway seeds
Parmesan cheese
bread crumbs
½ can tomato sauce

Cut zucchini into chunks; put in pan with small amount of water, dash of salt and onion. Simmer 7 minutes. Drain well. Mash up but not completely. Add grated cheddar cheese, tomato sauce, caraway seeds. Put in casserole. Cover top with Parmesan cheese and bread crumbs. Bake at 350 degrees for ½ hour.

FESTIVE ZUCCHINI

½ cup chopped onion
¼ cup oil
4 cups sliced zucchini
1 cup thinly sliced green pepper strips
¼ teaspoon salt
⅛ teaspoon pepper
1 tablespoon chopped pimiento

In large skillet, sauté onion in oil until tender. Stir in zucchini, green pepper, salt and pepper. Cover and cook over medium heat 10 minutes or until zucchini is tender, stirring occasionally. Serve garnished with chopped pimiento. Makes 6 servings.

SUMMER SQUASH CASSEROLE

1 pound summer squash, grated
1 egg
¾ cup rolled crackers (not soda crackers)
garlic purée or 1 small fresh garlic clove, crushed
2 tablespoons butter or margarine
salt, pepper, parsley to taste

Butter casserole dish (1 ½ quart size). Mix all ingredients except butter and pour into casserole dish. Dot top with butter. Cover and bake for 1 hour at 350 degrees.

May be prepared ahead, refrigerated, and then cooked just prior to serving. Serves 5-6.

PICKLED BEETS

1 bunch beets
vinegar and beet stock to cover, half and half
1 tablespoon sugar
1 teaspoon whole allspice
1 medium onion, sliced

Cut off the tops of the beets, leaving 1-inch of stem.
Wash very thoroughly. Cook in boiling, salted water until
tender. Skin and slice. Pour beet stock and vinegar over.
Add sugar, allspice, and onion; let stand. If the beets are
warm they will be pickled in ½ hour, but the longer you
leave them in the marinade, the better. Serve cold.

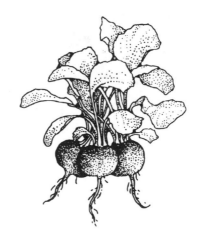

HEARTY LENTIL STEW

1 potato, peeled and cubed
2 medium onions, peeled and chopped
¼ pound mushrooms, sliced
1 clove garlic, chopped
1 medium carrot, peeled and sliced
2 stalks celery, chopped
1½ cups lentils, rinsed and drained
1 (16-ounce) can tomatoes, undrained and crushed
2 cups beef broth
1 cup water
½ cup dry red wine
1 small bay leaf
1 tablespoon Worcestershire sauce
½ teaspoon thyme
½ teaspoon marjoram
¼ teaspoon black pepper
¼ teaspoon chervil
¼ teaspoon caraway seeds

Lightly brown potato, onions, mushrooms, garlic, carrot and celery in non-stick skillet sprayed with vegetable coating. Add lentils, tomatoes, broth, water, wine, bay leaf, Worcestershire, thyme, marjoram, pepper, chervil and caraway seeds.

Simmer, partly covered, adding water as needed, 1 to 1 ½ hours, until vegetables and lentils are tender. Makes 6 servings.

SICILIAN VEGETABLE CASSEROLE

2 packages frozen Italian green beans
2 packages peas
2 cans artichokes
2 cups sliced mushrooms
1 cup sliced onion
salt and pepper
garlic powder to taste
¼ cup Italian bread crumbs
¼ cup Parmesan cheese
½ cup red wine
¼ cup olive oil

Oil a large casserole and layer with each of the listed vegetables. Sprinkle bread crumbs, Parmesan cheese, salt, pepper, and garlic powder. Repeat layers.

On top sprinkle red wine and olive oil. Bake at 400 degrees for 1 ½ hours. Recipe may be cut in half.

CREAMED SPINACH

1 (10-ounce) package frozen chopped spinach
2 bacon slices, finely chopped
½ cup finely chopped onion
2 tablespoons flour
1 teaspoon seasoned salt
¼ teaspoon seasoned pepper
1 clove garlic, minced
1 cup milk

Cook spinach according to package directions, but omit salt. Drain well. Fry bacon and onion together until onion is tender, about 10 minutes. Remove from heat. Add flour, seasoned salt, seasoned pepper and garlic. Blend thoroughly. Slowly add milk, return to heat and stir until thickened. Add spinach and mix thoroughly. Makes 4 servings.

STEWED TOMATOES

boiling water
3 large tomatoes, about 1½ pounds
1 bay leaf
1 tablespoon butter or margarine
1 tablespoon sugar
½ teaspoon salt
⅛ teaspoon pepper

Pour boiling water over tomatoes; let stand for 1 minute. Drain and cover with cold water. Peel the skin off and cut into cubes, measuring 3½ cups. In medium saucepan, combine tomatoes with remaining ingredients and bring to a boil. Reduce heat and simmer, covered, about 8 minutes, or until tomatoes are tender.

STUFFED TOMATOES

6 large ripe tomatoes
1 cup lump crabmeat
½ cup chopped celery
½ teaspoon salt
white pepper to taste
¼ cup mayonnaise, or to taste
1 hard-cooked egg, chopped
1 tablespoon minced parsley
paprika

Hollow out the tomatoes, removing the stem end. Mix crabmeat and celery with salt, pepper, and mayonnaise. Stuff the tomatoes with the mixture. Sprinkle with chopped egg and top each with a little parsley and a dash of paprika.

Sauces
Dressings

BUTTERMILK ORANGE DRESSING

2 tablespoons orange juice
1½ tablespoons white wine vinegar
2 teaspoons Dijon mustard
2 tablespoons mayonnaise
¼ cup vegetable oil
¼ cup buttermilk*
1 teaspoon grated orange peel
salt and pepper to taste

Mix together orange juice, vinegar, mustard and mayonnaise. Whisk in oil and buttermilk. Stir in orange zest and season with salt and pepper.

*Plain yogurt can be substituted for buttermilk.

FRENCH DRESSING

¼ cup water
¼ cup red wine vinegar
¼ teaspoon sugar
1½ teaspoons lemon juice
½ teaspoon salt
½ teaspoon Worcestershire sauce
¾ teaspoon dry mustard
½ clove garlic, minced
¼ cup olive oil
¾ cup vegetable oil

Combine all ingredients and chill. Shake well before using. Makes 1½ cups of dressing.

CURRY DRESSING

¾ cup mayonnaise
1½ tablespoons curry powder
1½ tablespoons prepared mustard
¼ cup lemon juice
5 cloves garlic, minced or pressed
4-ounces sharp cheddar cheese

Combine mayonnaise, curry powder, mustard, lemon juice, and garlic in a bowl. Blend well. Stir in cheddar cheese.

HONEY MUSTARD DRESSING

¼ cup vinegar
¾-1 cup mayonnaise
2 teaspoons prepared mustard
1 teaspoon sugar
2 teaspoons chopped onion
½ cup honey
1 teaspoon minced parsley
salt, pepper
½ cup oil

Mix vinegar, mayonnaise and mustard until smooth. Add sugar, onion, honey and parsley. Season to taste with salt and pepper. Slowly add oil until well blended. Makes 2 cups.

COCKTAIL SAUCE

1 cup catsup
1 tablespoon white horseradish, grated
2 teaspoons lemon juice
Tabasco sauce to taste
Worcestershire sauce to taste

Combine all ingredients.

LAMAZE SAUCE

1 cup mayonnaise
1 cup chili sauce
1 cup India relish, well drained
1 teaspoon prepared mustard
1 teaspoon Worcestershire sauce
1 tablespoon prepared horseradish
dash Tabasco
1 hard-cooked egg, chopped
fresh ground black pepper
1 pimiento, chopped
1 tablespoon chopped chives
1 teaspoon Escoffier Sauce Diable, optional

Mix all ingredients together thoroughly. Refrigerate until needed. Makes about 3 cups sauce.

EGG BATTER

1 cup milk
1 egg
½ teaspoon salt

Beat all ingredients together.

HOLLANDAISE SAUCE

½ cup butter or margarine
3 egg yolks
2 tablespoons lemon juice
¼ teaspoon salt
dash red pepper
⅛ cup boiling water
1 tablespoon chopped green onion or chives
1 teaspoon chopped parsley

Melt butter and keep warm. Combine egg yolks, lemon juice, salt and red pepper in blender. With blender running, slowly add butter, the hot water. Pour mixture into saucepan and cook and stir over low heat until thickened. Fold in green onion and parsley.

MARINARA SAUCE

4 large cans crushed tomatoes
2 large cloves fresh garlic, chopped
¼ -⅓ cup oil
1 handful of fresh parsley, chopped
1 teaspoon sugar
½ cup red wine
salt and pepper to taste

Put oil in large pot. Add garlic and sauté in hot oil for a few minutes or until light brown. Add tomatoes, parsley, sugar, wine, salt and pepper. Simmer 1 ½ hours.

TARTAR SAUCE

1 cup mayonnaise
1 tablespoon minced onion
1 tablespoon minced parsley
1 tablespoon chopped olives (optional)
2 tablespoons green pickle relish, well drained

Mix all ingredients together well and refrigerate for several hours before serving. Makes about 1 cup of sauce.

PESTO SAUCE

2 cups packed lettuce leaf basil
2 cups packed dark opal basil
¼ cup chopped Italian parsley
¼ cup freshly grated Parmesan cheese
¼ cup freshly grated Romano cheese
¼ cup extra virgin olive oil
¼ cup unsalted butter, softened
2 cloves garlic, finely chopped
½ teaspoon salt
dash freshly ground black pepper
¾ teaspoon Marsala wine
¾ teaspoon dry red wine
¾ teaspoon dry white wine
¾ tablespoon pine nuts, toasted and finely chopped

Place basils in blender or food processor and chop. Add parsley, Parmesan and Romano cheeses, olive oil, butter, garlic, salt, pepper, Marsala, red and white wines and pine nuts and process to blend with basil. Makes about 1 ½-cups sauce.

BASIL

LOBSTER SAUCE

3 tablespoons butter
3 tablespoons flour
1 teaspoon salt
dash freshly ground pepper
1 cup milk
½ cup cream
¼ cup dry sherry
1-1½ cups cooked, diced lobster

Melt the butter. Add the flour, salt, and pepper; stir to blend smoothly. Continue cooking over medium heat. Pour milk and cream in gradually, stirring constantly until the sauce thickens. Reduce heat and cook gently for 2 minutes. Add sherry and lobster and let cook just long enough to heat through. Makes 3 cups of sauce.

SPICY SHRIMP MARINADE

1 cup rice wine vinegar
¼ cup lime juice
½ cup olive oil
2 tablespoons chopped cilantro
2 cloves garlic, minced
1 teaspoon sesame oil
salt
1 teaspoon red chili paste, or to taste

Combine vinegar, lime juice, olive oil, cilantro, garlic, sesame oil, and salt to taste. Add 1 teaspoon chili paste or more to taste.

SHRIMP NEWBURG SAUCE

1 tablespoon butter
1 teaspoon flour
1 cup heavy cream
salt and pepper
cayenne pepper
½ cup chopped, cooked shrimp
2 egg yolks
3 tablespoons sherry

Melt the butter. Stir in flour and blend until smooth. Add cream and stir until hot and well blended. Add salt and pepper to taste and a few grains of cayenne pepper. Add shrimp and heat, but do not boil. Add a little of the sauce to the egg yolks and beat well. Add to the sauce, together with the sherry. Stir well and heat, but *do not boil.*

Pasta

ANGEL HAIR PASTA WITH PINE NUTS

3 shallots, chopped
4 green onions, sliced
2 tablespoons olive oil
¼ pound mushrooms, sliced
2 zucchinis, sliced
½ red bell pepper, sliced
¼ cup balsamic vinegar
dash red pepper flakes
½ teaspoon chervil
¾ cup sun-dried tomatoes, from the jar
  with oil
½ cup pine nuts, toasted
10-12-ounces angel hair pasta

Heat oil in large pan. Add shallots and onions and sauté just until tender. Add mushrooms, zucchinis, and bell pepper and sauté until crisp, about 5 minutes. Add vinegar, red pepper flakes, chervil, and sun-dried tomatoes and cook a few minutes longer.

Meanwhile, cook pasta according to package directions; drain and rinse. Toss in pine nuts with vegetable mixture. Toss with pasta. Makes 4-5 servings.

BROCCOLI AND MUSHROOM FETTUCCINE

1 bunch broccoli (1¾ pounds), cut in 1½-inch pieces
2 medium zucchini, cut into ¼-inch slices
1 pound fettuccine
½ cup olive oil
2 large cloves of garlic, peeled and minced
½ pound mushrooms, sliced
½ teaspoon salt
1 cup minced Italian parsley
1 tablespoon lemon juice
4 tablespoons unsalted butter, sliced into pats
1 cup fresh grated Parmesan cheese
½ cup whipping cream, room temperature
¼ teaspoon nutmeg

Remove the thick broccoli stalks and save for another use. Bring 3½ quarts water to a boil in a large pot. Add 1 tablespoon salt. Drop in broccoli and zucchini. Let water boil again. Boil 30 seconds or until vegetables are bright green, just done and crisp. Drain immediately in colander; rinse with cold running water to cool off. Set aside. Meanwhile, bring 6 quarts of water to boil for pasta. Add 1½ tablespoons salt. While pasta is cooking, heat olive oil in a 12-14-inch skillet. When hot, put in garlic. Stir for a few seconds. Add mushrooms. Stir for about 1 minute; add drained broccoli and zucchini. Stir for another minute. Add parsley, ½ teaspoon salt or to taste, ground pepper and lemon juice. Stir and cook for 30 seconds. Turn off heat under the skillet.

Drain pasta and empty it into large bowl. Add butter and cheese and toss. Add cream, nutmeg and toss again. Empty contents of skillet, including oily juices over pasta.

Toss lightly and serve. Makes 6 servings.

CRAB PASTA CASSEROLE

¼ cup butter or margarine
1 medium onion, chopped
¼ pound mushrooms, sliced
1 large clove garlic, minced
10-12-ounces conchiglie (seashell pasta)
boiling salted water
¾ pound cooked fresh or canned crab
⅓ cup sliced stuffed green olives
4-ounces grated sharp cheddar cheese
¼ cup sour cream
1 large can tomatoes with juice, chopped
½ teaspoon basil
dash red pepper

Melt butter in a frying pan over medium heat. Add onions, mushrooms, and garlic and cook about 5 minutes. Meanwhile boil water, add salt and pasta and cook until al dente. Drain pasta and put in oven-proof casserole dish. Add onion mixture, crab, olives, cheese, sour cream, tomatoes and their liquid, basil, and pepper. Bake uncovered in a 350 degree oven for 30-35 minutes. Makes 4 servings.

LINGUINE WITH SHRIMP

3 white onions, sliced thin
2 cloves garlic, minced
3 tablespoons olive oil
8 large ripe tomatoes, fresh or canned,
  cut up
2 teaspoons salt
1 teaspoon sugar
1 cup white wine
1 pound raw shrimp, shelled and deveined
2 tablespoons chopped parsley
12-ounces linguine

Sauté onions and garlic in oil until soft and golden brown.
Add cut up tomatoes, salt and sugar. Simmer 25
minutes. In another pot, bring wine to boil and drop in
shrimp and simmer 3 minutes until pink; add to tomato
sauce. Stir in parsley and cook 5 minutes. Cook linguine,
drain, and pour sauce over. Serves 4.

MEDITERRANEAN PASTA

¾ cup green pepper, julienned
¾ cup red bell pepper, julienned
½ cup black olives, pitted and sliced
2 tablespoons olive oil
⅛ cup chicken broth
⅔ cup mozzarella cheese
3 tablespoons Parmesan cheese
1½ cups *Marinara Sauce*, see page 72
12-16 ounces penne pasta
½-¾ pound shrimp, cooked, optional

Sauté vegetables in oil until just tender, about 5 minutes. Add chicken broth and simmer 5 minutes longer. Add *Marinara Sauce*. If using seafood, add at this point and heat through.

Meanwhile, cook pasta according to package instructions. Add pasta and cheeses and mix well. Serves 5-6.

NOODLE PUDDING

1 pound fine egg noodles
1 ½ pints sour cream
½ cup sugar
1 teaspoon salt
3 beaten eggs
1 pound cream cheese
1 pound cottage cheese
½ cup raisins, optional
Topping

Mix all ingredients together except for ½ pint sour cream. Pour into 9x13 baking dish and spread rest of sour cream on top. Bake in preheated 325 degree oven for 1 ½ hours. Spread on topping and bake ½ hour longer.

TOPPING

½ cup brown sugar
2 tablespoons flour
2 teaspoons cinnamon
2 tablespoons softened butter

Mix all ingredients together.

PASTA WITH LOBSTER AND TARRAGON*

2 tablespoons olive oil
¾ cup finely chopped yellow onion
1 large and 1 small can Italian plum tomatoes
3 teaspoons dried tarragon
1 cup heavy cream
2 tablespoons salt
1 pound spaghetti or fettuccine, cooked
pinch cayenne pepper
1½ cups lobster meat or more
salt and fresh pepper
garnish with parsley, fresh basil, or fresh tarragon sprigs

Heat the oil in a saucepan. Add the onion; reduce the heat and cook covered until tender, about 25 minutes. Chop and drain the tomatoes; add them to the onions. Add the tarragon, season to taste with salt and pepper; bring to a boil. Reduce heat; cover and simmer for 30 minutes, stirring occasionally. Remove the mixture from the heat and let it cool slightly. Purée it in the bowl of a food processor fitted with a steel blade. Return purée to the saucepan, stir in heavy cream and set over medium heat. Stirring often, simmer the mixture for 15 minutes or until slightly reduced. Correct for seasonings. Stir in cayenne and lobster meat. Simmer further for 3-5 minutes or just until lobster is heated through.

To cook pasta, bring 4 quarts salted water to a boil in a large pot. Stir in the pasta and cook until al dente. Drain immediately and arrange on warm serving plates. Spoon sauce evenly over pasta and garnish with a sprig of parsley, basil or tarragon. Serve immediately. Serves 6-8.

*Shrimp can be substituted for lobster.

PASTA WITH SALMON

½ pound penne pasta
1 teaspoon butter
1 medium yellow onion, peeled and thinly sliced
salt, pepper
10-ounce salmon fillet, cut in 1-inch squares
¼ cup white wine
2 cups half-and-half or whipping cream
1 ¼ tablespoons chopped parsley
freshly ground pepper

Cook pasta in boiling, salted water until tender. Drain in colander and rinse in cold running water. Leave in cold water in pot. Set aside. Melt butter in skillet until bubbly. Add onion, season to taste with salt and pepper and sauté until onion is transparent. Add salmon and white wine. Cook salmon 1 minute; do not allow to turn pink. Remove salmon. Continue cooking until wine is reduced by half. Add cream and reduce mixture by ⅓, or until it coats metal spoon. Add salmon.

When ready to serve, submerge pasta in boiling water until heated through. Strain and place in bowl large enough to toss with sauce (reheat if necessary). Garnish with chopped parsley. Season to taste with freshly ground pepper. Serves 4.

SHRIMP WITH FETTUCCINE

1 clove garlic, minced
4 tablespoons butter or margarine
¾ cup sliced asparagus or broccoli
¾ cup peas, optional
½ cup sliced green onions
¾ pound shrimp, cooked
2 tablespoons minced parsley
½ teaspoon basil
⅛ teaspoon crushed, dried hot red pepper
2 tablespoons dry white wine
8-ounces fettuccine, cooked and drained
2 tablespoons grated Parmesan cheese
¼ teaspoon salt
⅛ teaspoon black pepper

In large skillet, cook garlic in butter. Add asparagus, peas and green onions; cook and stir about 5 minutes or until vegetables are tender but still crisp. Stir in shrimp, parsley, basil, red pepper and wine. Cook and stir over high heat 1 minute or until shrimp is heated through. Serve over hot fettuccine. Sprinkle with Parmesan cheese, salt and pepper. Makes 4 servings.

SPINACH GORGONZOLA FETTUCCINE

2 tablespoons olive oil
1 large clove garlic, minced
2 cups (4-ounces) torn fresh spinach
½ cup (2-ounces) Gorgonzola cheese
¼ cup coarsely chopped walnuts
6-ounces cooked fettuccine
white pepper

Heat olive oil in large skillet. Add garlic and cook over low heat 5 minutes. Add spinach and cook over medium heat until tender, about 5 minutes, stirring frequently.

Stir in cheese and nuts. Add cooked fettuccine and toss well to melt cheese into spinach and pasta. Season well with white pepper. Makes 2 servings.

TORTELLINI WITH EGGPLANT

1 (9-ounce) package tortellini
2 cloves garlic, minced
2 Japanese eggplants, thinly sliced
2 tablespoons oil
Marinara Sauce, approximately 2 pints, see page 72
1 (5½-ounce) package goat cheese
2 tablespoons basil leaves, cut into strips

Cook tortellini according to package directions; drain well.
Heat oil in large skillet until hot. Add eggplant slices in
single layer. Brown on both sides. Remove slices and
keep warm while browning remaining batches. Add
additional oil if needed. Add garlic while browning last
batch of eggplant. Return all eggplant to skillet. Stir in
Marinara Sauce and heat to simmering. Cut goat cheese
into cubes and add to skillet, pushing down into sauce.
Cover and heat several minutes, just until cheese begins
to soften. Sprinkle basil over top. Makes 3-4 servings.

VEGETABLE FETTUCCINE CARBONARA

1 egg
¼ cup whipping cream
8 slices bacon, chopped
½ cup sliced mushrooms
2½ cups sliced carrot
½ cup sliced cauliflower
½ cup frozen peas, thawed
½ cup zucchini, sliced
½ red bell pepper, seeded and cut into 1-inch strips
¼ cup sliced green onion
1 garlic clove, chopped
12-ounce package fettuccine
¼ cup butter or margarine, cut into pieces
1 cup freshly grated Parmesan cheese
salt and ground pepper

Beat eggs with cream in small bowl and set aside. Cook bacon in heavy large skillet until crisp. Remove with slotted spoon and set aside. Add mushrooms, carrots, cauliflower, peas, zucchini, red pepper, onion and garlic to skillet and sauté until crisp-tender, about 5 to 7 minutes.

Cook fettuccine in large amount of boiling, salted water until al dente. Drain well. Transfer to large serving bowl. Add butter and toss through. Add vegetables, bacon and cheese and toss again. Season with salt pepper. Serve hot. Makes 4 servings.

Poultry Meat

HONEY BAKED CHICKEN

3-4 pounds chicken, cut up
½ cup butter or margarine, melted
½ cup honey
¼ cup prepared mustard
1 teaspoon curry powder

Place chicken pieces in shallow baking dish, skin side up (chicken may be skinned). Combine rest of ingredients and pour over chicken and bake at 350 degrees 1¼ hours, basting every 15 minutes until chicken is golden brown and tender. Serves 4.

CHICKEN MARENGO

2 frying chickens cut into quarters
½ cup dry white wine
½ teaspoon thyme
2 cups Italian style tomatoes
20 small pearl onions
juice of one lemon
1 thinly sliced onion
½ cup olive oil
3 cloves crushed garlic
1 cup chicken broth
1 pound sliced mushrooms
¼ cup butter or margarine
1 can pitted black olives, sliced
1½-ounces cognac

Sauté onion lightly in olive oil and remove. Add chicken

and brown well on all sides. Add white wine, thyme, tomatoes, garlic, and chicken broth. Cover and simmer 1 hour and remove chicken from sauce.

Strain sauce and reduce by cooking 5 minutes. Sauté lemon, pearl onions, and mushrooms in butter. Combine chicken, mushrooms, onions, and sliced olives in casserole dish. Sprinkle with cognac. Add reduced sauce and put in 350 degree oven to reheat.

CHICKEN PESTO

2 boneless, skinless chicken breasts, cut into
  bite-size pieces
prepared pesto sauce, or see page 73
1 tablespoon oil
garlic salt to taste
rottele pasta

Place oil in frying pan with a little of the pesto sauce and heat. Sauté chicken quickly until just undercooked. Add garlic salt to taste.

Boil water and cook rottele. Add to the chicken mixture along with rest of pesto sauce.

Optional: add cooked vegetables to chicken, such as broccoli or asparagus.

ALMOND CHICKEN SAUTÉ

4 chicken breast halves, skinned
boiling water
2 tablespoons flour
salt to taste
¼ teaspoon black pepper
3 tablespoons margarine
1 tablespoon oil
1½ tablespoons lemon juice
1 red apple, cored and cut into thin wedges
½ cup whole almonds, toasted
½ cup dry white wine
¼ cup sliced green onions
1 tablespoon Italian parsley, chopped

Place chicken in saucepan. Cover with boiling water. Bring to boil and cook, covered, 2 minutes. Drain chicken and pat dry with paper towels. Combine flour, pepper and salt if desired. Dust chicken with flour mixture on both sides. Heat 2 tablespoons margarine and oil in skillet over medium-high heat. Add chicken and brown 3 minutes on each side. Add lemon juice to skillet. Reduce heat to medium and cook, covered, until chicken is tender and juices run clear, about 5 minutes on each side. Transfer chicken to platter and keep warm.

Melt remaining 1 tablespoon butter in skillet over medium heat. Add apple and cook 2 minutes. Stir in almonds, wine, and onions. Bring to a boil.

Cook, stirring constantly, 1 minute to loosen brown bits. Continue heating just long enough to reduce liquid slightly, then spoon mixture over chicken. Garnish with parsley.

CHICKEN KELLY

3 whole chicken breasts, skinned, boned, and halved
2 eggs, slightly beaten
1 cup bread crumbs, seasoned
1 tablespoon parsley flakes
½ teaspoon garlic powder
olive oil
1 tablespoon margarine
¾-1 pound sliced mushrooms
sliced Muenster cheese
2 cubes chicken bouillon
1 cup water or ½ cup water and ½ cup white wine

Marinate chicken in eggs for 2 hours. Mix crumbs, parsley, garlic in bag. Add chicken one piece at a time and shake. Brown in a little oil and drain on paper towel. Melt margarine in 9X13 pan. Add chicken and layer of mushrooms; cover with cheese. Dissolve bouillon in hot water or combination water and wine. Pour over casserole. Bake uncovered in 350 degree oven for 30-45 minutes.

PARSLEY

SOCIETY HILL CHICKEN

8 large chicken breasts, halved and skinned
several cloves of garlic, peeled and chopped fine
¼ cup dried oregano or tarragon
salt and freshly ground pepper to taste
½ cup red wine vinegar
½ cup olive oil
1 cup pitted prunes, cut up
½ cup stuffed green olives
½ cup capers with a little juice
6 bay leaves
1 cup brown sugar
1 cup white wine
¼ cup cilantro or parsley, finely chopped

In a large bowl combine all ingredients except sugar, wine and cilantro. Add chicken breasts, cover, and refrigerate overnight.

The next day, arrange chicken breasts in a single layer in large shallow baking pans and spoon marinade over them. Sprinkle with brown sugar and pour wine around them. Bake in a preheated 350 degree oven for 30-45 minutes or until done, basting frequently. Chicken is done when juices run clear when pierced with a fork.

Remove to serving dish and sprinkle with cilantro or parsley. Pass remaining pan juice. May be served cold.

CHICKEN POT PIE

2 cups diced cooked chicken
½ cup diced celery
2 medium onions, diced
2 medium potatoes, diced
½ cup shelled peas
5 tablespoons chicken fat
4 tablespoons flour
1 tablespoon powdered chicken stock base
2½ cups chicken stock
salt and pepper
flaky pie crust or biscuit dough

Cook the vegetables and drain well. Arrange chicken and vegetables in four individual dishes. Melt the chicken fat, add flour, and stir until smooth. Add powdered chicken stock base and chicken stock and stir constantly until smooth and thickened. Season to taste with salt and pepper. Pour gravy over the meat and vegetables and top with pie crust. Seal well at the edges and prick in the center to allow steam to escape. Bake in a 400 degree oven 25 to 30 minutes, or until crust is nicely browned. Serves 4.

RICOTTA-STUFFED CHICKEN BREASTS

2 cups ricotta cheese
1 (10-ounce) package frozen chopped spinach,
  thawed, drained, and squeezed dry
1 egg
½ cup freshly grated Parmesan cheese
½ cup grated Swiss cheese
2 garlic cloves, minced
½ teaspoon salt
¼ teaspoon freshly ground pepper
4 chicken breast halves, boned, skin intact
butter
freshly cooked rice or spinach pasta

Preheat oven to 350 degrees. Combine first 8 ingredients in medium bowl and mix thoroughly. Rinse chicken breasts and pat dry. Pound slightly to even thickness. Carefully separate skin from chicken using fingers or small paring knife, leaving skin attached on one long side to form pocket. Divide stuffing among pockets, patting gently to distribute evenly. Secure with toothpicks.

Arrange chicken, skin side up, in baking dish. Dot with butter. Bake until juices run clear when pierced with a fork, basting with pan drippings every 10 minutes, about 30-35 minutes. Serve immediately over rice or pasta.

CHICKEN WITH MUSHROOMS

¼ cup flour
¼ teaspoon salt
dash pepper
4 tablespoons butter or margarine
3-4 chicken breasts, halved, skinned and boned
⅓-½ pound mushrooms, sliced
¼ cup thinly sliced green onions
½ cup chicken broth
3 tablespoons sherry

Mix the flour, salt and pepper in a shallow dish or pan. Melt the butter in a very large frying pan over medium heat. Dredge the chicken pieces in the flour mixture and brown both sides lightly in the butter. Remove from the butter and set aside. Save the remaining flour mixture (you will need ¾ tablespoon of it). Add the mushrooms and green onions to the butter and sauté until they start to soften. Sprinkle with the ¾ tablespoon flour. Stir in the broth and sherry. Return the chicken to the pan and simmer, uncovered, for about 10 to 15 minutes or until the chicken is done and the sauce has thickened. Correct for seasonings. Serves 3-4.

CITRUS SESAME CHICKEN

2 cups breadcrumbs
¾ cup sesame seeds
½ cup freshly grated Parmesan cheese
¼ cup chopped fresh parsley
1 teaspoon freshly ground white pepper
6 chicken breasts, skinned, split, boned and pounded
   to ¼-inch thickness
2 tablespoons butter or margarine, melted
Sauce

Preheat oven to 375 degrees. Combine first 5 ingredients in medium bowl and blend well. Dip chicken breasts in butter and then coat with sesame breading. Place on baking sheet and bake 20-30 minutes. Serve immediately with warm sauce.

SAUCE

3 oranges
3 lemons
1 cup red currant jelly
3 tablespoons port
3 teaspoons Dijon mustard
¼ teaspoon ground ginger or nutmeg
dash red pepper

Finely grate, peel, and squeeze juice from oranges and lemons. Place peel in large saucepan, cover with cold water and bring to boil. Drain. Repeat this process twice. Combine juice and remaining ingredients in small saucepan and heat through. Stir in grated peel to taste.

ROSEMARY CHICKEN

12 chicken breast halves, skinned
½ cup extra-virgin olive oil
¼ cup chopped rosemary
salt, pepper
6 tablespoons dry white wine
2 shallots, minced
½ cup butter
juice of 2 medium lemons
¼ cup chopped Italian parsley

Brush chicken breasts with olive oil and sprinkle with rosemary. Season to taste with salt and pepper. Place under hot broiler or on barbecue grill and cook 3 to 4 minutes on each side or until just done.

To prepare sauce, combine white wine and shallots in saucepan and cook over high heat until liquid is reduced to half. Add butter, lemon juice, parsley, and salt and pepper to taste. When butter is partially melted, remove from heat and whip to thicken slightly. Pour some sauce over chicken breasts and serve the rest on the side. Makes 6 servings.

ROSEMARY

CHICKEN PICCATA

6 (6-ounce) boneless, skinless chicken breasts
flour
½ cup margarine or combination of
  olive oil and margarine
½ cup dry white wine
juice of 2 lemons
salt, pepper
¼ cup chopped parsley
2 tablespoons capers, optional

Dredge chicken breasts in flour to coat both sides. Melt margarine over low heat. Do not let butter brown. Add chicken and cook 5 minutes, turning to brown both sides. Add wine, half the lemon juice and season to taste with salt and pepper. Sprinkle parsley and capers over chicken.

Cover and simmer 5 to 7 minutes longer or until chicken is done. Sprinkle with remaining lemon juice. Place chicken on platter and pour pan juices over chicken. Makes 6 servings.

PARSLEY

TURKEY TETRAZZINI

2 cups diced cooked turkey
½ pound spaghetti
½ pound mushrooms
4 tablespoons butter
2 tablespoons flour
1 cup chicken or turkey stock
1 cup cream of half-and-half
2 tablespoons sherry
salt and pepper to taste
grated Parmesan cheese

Break up the spaghetti and cook 9 minutes in boiling, salted water; drain well. Slice the mushrooms with stems and sauté in butter 5 minutes. Sprinkle the flour over the mushrooms and stir to blend well. Add stock and cream and cook over medium heat, stirring constantly, until thickened. Add sherry and season to taste with salt and pepper. Add turkey and heat through. Line a baking dish with the spaghetti and pour the turkey mixture into the center. Sprinkle liberally with grated Parmesan cheese and bake in a 400 degree oven until top is golden (20 to 25 minutes). Serves 4.

SPRING LAMB STEW

3 tablespoons butter
3 pounds lamb shoulder or breast, cut in squares
3 small onions, sliced
2 tablespoons flour
2¼ cups chicken or beef broth
1 teaspoon salt
½ teaspoon black pepper
2 teaspoons rosemary
1 crushed clove garlic
1 bay leaf
1 pound new potatoes, as small as you can find
1½ cups diced carrots
¾ cup diced turnip
1½ pounds frozen small peas

Melt butter in stew pot. Brown meat over medium heat, remove and then brown onions. Remove onions, fry flour in butter until light brown, then slowly add broth, stirring until smooth.

Return meat and onions to pot with salt, pepper, rosemary, garlic and bay leaf. Simmer covered until meat is nearly cooked, about 1 hour.

Add potatoes, carrots and turnip and cook slowly for another 35 to 40 minutes. Then add peas and cook until done. Makes 6 servings.

TENDERLOIN STEW

2 medium skirt steaks
fresh ground pepper
paprika
1 can beef consommé soup
1 package dry onion soup
3 carrots
Optional: green pepper, potatoes

Slice steaks into ½-inch slices. In heavy pot, brown meat with pepper and paprika. Add other ingredients. Cover and simmer for 45 to 60 minutes. Can be served over noodles or rice if potatoes are not used. Serves 2-3.

FLORENTINE CUBE STEAKS

1 small onion, chopped
1 tablespoon butter or margarine
1 (10-ounce) package frozen chopped spinach,
  thawed and drained
¼ cup shredded mozzarella cheese
1 tablespoon grated Parmesan cheese
4 cubed steaks
1 tablespoon flour
½ tablespoon flour
½ teaspoon salt
⅛ teaspoon black pepper
2 tablespoons oil
¼ cup water

Cook onion in butter until transparent. Add spinach,
mozzarella and Parmesan. Heat briefly to warm spinach.
Toss lightly. Divide spinach mixture into 4 equal portions.
Place one portion down center of each steak. Bring sides
of steak up to overlap and enclose filling. Secure with
wood picks.

Combine flour, salt and pepper. Dredge steak rolls.
Slowly brown in oil in large skillet 10-12 minutes. Pour
off drippings; add water, cover tightly and bring to boil.
Reduce heat and simmer until done, about 5 minutes.
Makes 4 servings.

BRAISED SHORT RIBS

4 pounds short ribs
salt and pepper
flour
½ cup diced celery
1 clove garlic, mashed
2 tablespoons chopped onion

Season the ribs with salt and pepper and dredge them lightly with flour. Place in a 450 degree oven and brown well (about 15 minutes). Reduce heat to 350 degrees.

Mix celery, garlic, and onion and spread the mixture over the meat. Add a little water to the pan and return it to the oven. Roast, basting occasionally and adding more water to the pan if necessary, for 1 hour, or until tender. Serve with pan gravy. Serves 4.

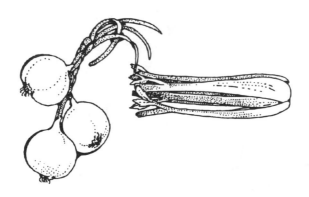

MARINATED SKIRT STEAK

6 skirt steaks, trimmed of fat
¼ cup canola oil
¼ cup light soy sauce
½ cup rice vinegar
¼ cup orange juice
½ cup pineapple juice
1 medium onion, coarsely chopped
¼ cup hot mustard, such as *Old Original Bookbinder's Horseradish Mustard*

Place skirt steaks in non-aluminum pan in single layer. Combine all other ingredients and pour mixture over steaks. Marinate 12 to 24 hours. Remove from marinade and cook steaks over medium-low coals or under broiler 4-inches from source of heat to desired doneness; overcooking may cause steak to be tough.

MEATLOAF

4 slices bread
½ cup milk
2 eggs
2 pounds ground round
¼ cup chopped onion
2 tablespoons chopped celery
2 teaspoons salt
½ teaspoon poultry seasoning
¼ teaspoon pepper
¼ teaspoon dry mustard
1 tablespoon Worcestershire sauce

bread crumbs
chili sauce

Soak bread in milk and beat with eggs. Mix meat with all ingredients except bread crumbs. Form into two loaves and roll in bread crumbs. Paint with chili sauce and place in a greased baking dish. Pour boiling water around loaves and bake in a 375 degree oven for 50 minutes. Serves 6.

Serving Suggestion: halfway through cooking, add 1 large can of whole new potatoes; continue baking, basting often.

PRIME RIB

1 prime rib roast
2 cloves garlic
salt and pepper
1 to 2 medium onions, thinly sliced

Wipe roast with damp paper towel. Rub roast with garlic cloves and season to taste with salt and pepper. Place onion slices over fatty top side of roast.

Place meat in roasting pan. Roast at 500 degrees about 20 minutes, then reduce heat to 325 degrees. Cook 8 to 11 minutes per pound for rare to medium-rare; 15 to 18 minutes per pound for medium; and 30 to 35 minutes per pound for well done. If you use a meat thermometer, it should read 140 degrees for rare; 160 degrees for medium; and 170 degrees for well done.

STUFFED BELL PEPPERS

4 green peppers
2 tablespoons minced onion
2 tablespoons minced celery
1 tablespoon butter
1 pound chopped sirloin
2 cups cooked rice
1 tablespoon powdered beef stock
1 egg, beaten
¼ cup bread crumbs
¼ cup milk
salt and pepper to taste
¼ cup chili sauce

Cut off and discard tops of peppers. Cut the peppers in half lengthwise and remove the seeds and membranes. Sauté onion and celery in butter until soft, but not brown. Add chopped beef and cook over medium heat, stirring constantly, until red color disappears. Mix well with all other ingredients and stuff into pepper halves. Place in greased baking dish. Bake in a 375 degree oven 20 to 25 minutes.

BEEF POT PIE

1 ½ pounds sirloin, cut in 1-inch cubes
flour
salt and pepper
2 tablespoons oil
1 tablespoon powdered beef stock
1 medium onion
1 bay leaf
½ cup diced celery
2 medium onions, diced
2 medium potatoes, diced
½ cup shelled peas
4 tablespoons butter
4 tablespoons flour
2 cups beef stock
flaky pie crust or biscuit dough

Dredge the beef cubes in flour seasoned with salt and pepper. Brown on all sides in hot oil. Cover with boiling water; add powdered beef stock, onion, and bay leaf, and simmer until tender (45 to 60 minutes). Cook the vegetables until they are just tender, and drain well. Arrange vegetables in four individual dishes. Melt the butter and blend in flour smoothly. Allow to brown. Add beef stock and stir constantly until thickened. Add cooked cubes of beef to this gravy and pour over the vegetables. Cover each dish with flaky pie crust or biscuit dough, sealing well at the edges, and prick the centers. Bake in a 400 degree oven 15 to 20 minutes, or until the crust is nicely browned. Serves 4.

VEAL PARMIGIANA

1¼ pounds thin veal cutlets
salt and pepper
1 egg
⅓ cup grated Parmesan cheese
⅓ cup bread crumbs
¼ cup olive oil
2 tablespoons butter
1 minced onion
1 can (6-ounce) tomato paste
2 cups hot water
½ teaspoon salt
½ teaspoon dried marjoram
½ teaspoon dried oregano
½ pound mozzarella cheese, sliced

Sprinkle veal with salt and pepper. Beat egg with 2 teaspoons water. Mix Parmesan cheese with bread crumbs. Dip veal in egg and roll in bread crumb mixture. Heat oil in large skillet. Sauté veal about 3 pieces at a time, until golden brown on each side. Lay in shallow, wide baking dish.

In same skillet sauté garlic until light brown; then add onion and cook until soft. Add tomato paste mixed with hot water, salt and marjoram. Boil a few minutes, scraping up all the brown from the bottom. Pour most of sauce over veal; add the cheese and then rest of sauce. Bake at 350 degrees for 30 minutes. Serves 3-4.

VEAL SCALOPPINE

1 ½ pounds veal cutlets
flour
salt and pepper
1 tablespoon butter
2 tablespoons olive oil
½ cup sliced onion
½ cup green pepper strips
2 tablespoons tomato purée
1 cup veal or chicken stock

Dredge the veal with flour and season with salt and pepper. Brown lightly in butter and oil. Add remaining ingredients, cover, and simmer for 20 to 30 minutes. Serves 4.

Seafood

BAKED FISH

If you are baking fish without a sauce, add a little *fish stock*, see page 17, to provide moisture and help prevent sticking. Bake fish from 8 to 12 minutes per pound, depending upon thickness and type of fish. The fish is done when it flakes easily with a fork.

For an easy and delicious way to prepare fish fillets, baste the fish with any of *Old Original Bookbinder's Bisque Soups* (diluted with milk or water). Sprinkle with fresh dill and pepper and either bake or broil until done.

BROILED FINNAN HADDIE

2 pounds finnan haddie
butter or margarine
paprika
pepper to taste

Steam the finnan haddie in very little water about 15 minutes. Drain. Remove center bone and place the fish in a shallow baking dish. Dot with butter and sprinkle with paprika. Add pepper to taste. Broil 3-inches from heat about 5 minutes. Serves 4.

CREAMED FINNAN HADDIE

1½ pounds finnan haddie
4 tablespoons margarine
4 tablespoons flour
2 cups light cream
salt and fresh ground pepper

Steam the fish in very little water until it flakes easily. Drain and flake. Melt the margarine. Blend in the flour, stirring until smooth. Add cream and continue cooking over medium heat, stirring constantly until thickened. Season to taste with salt and pepper. Add finnan haddie and heat through. Can be served on toast. Serves 3-4.

FLOUNDER FILLETS WITH TOMATO-HORSERADISH SAUCE

1 tablespoon olive oil
2 cups peeled, seeded and diced tomatoes
3 medium cloves garlic, minced
2 teaspoons dried oregano leaves, crushed
1 medium bay leaf
1 cup tomato juice
1 tablespoon balsamic vinegar
¼ teaspoon black pepper
2 tablespoons prepared horseradish
2 tablespoons unsalted butter, cut up
6 (4-ounce) flounder fillets
2 tablespoons chopped parsley

Heat oil in 10-inch skillet over medium heat. Add tomatoes, garlic, oregano and bay leaf and cook 10 minutes, stirring occasionally. Add tomato juice, vinegar and pepper. Simmer 20 minutes or until thickened. Discard bay leaf. Stir in horseradish and butter.

Meanwhile, arrange flounder in another 10-inch skillet. Cover with boiling water. Simmer 10 minutes or until fish flakes easily when tested with fork. Thin sauce with cooking liquid from fish to desired consistency. Sprinkle with parsley. Makes 6 servings.

FLOUNDER STUFFED WITH CRABMEAT

1 pound flounder fillets, preferably in 2 large pieces
salt and pepper
butter or margarine
½ pound lump crabmeat
¼ cup melted butter or margarine
dash cayenne pepper

Rinse fillets and pat dry. Place in a greased shallow baking dish. Season with salt and pepper and dot with butter. Broil 3-inches from heat for 3 minutes. Meanwhile, mix crabmeat with melted butter, salt, pepper, and cayenne pepper to taste. Remove fillets from broiler; turn one over and cover it with the crabmeat mixture. Top with the other fillet, browned side up. Dot with more butter and bake 10 minutes in a 350 degree oven. Serves 2-3.

COUNTRY HALIBUT

1 pound halibut steaks, thawed if necessary
2 tablespoons olive oil
1 tomato, diced
½ cup sliced mushrooms
¼ cup chopped onion
¼ cup chopped green pepper
⅓ cup dry white wine
1 tablespoon chopped parsley
1 clove garlic, crushed
½ teaspoon salt
¼ teaspoon black pepper
¼ teaspoon crushed thyme
1 bay leaf

In large skillet, lightly brown halibut in oil on both sides. Add all other ingredients. Bring to boil and simmer, covered, about 10 minutes or until halibut flakes easily when tested with fork. Remove halibut and vegetables to serving platter with slotted spoon. Keep warm. Simmer liquid until reduced to ¼ cup. Spoon over halibut. Makes 4 servings.

STUFFED HALIBUT STEAK

12 oysters
1 cup cracker crumbs
½ teaspoon salt
fresh ground pepper
1 tablespoon chopped parsley
2 tablespoons melted butter
2 halibut steaks, about 1½ pounds each
1 tablespoon lemon juice
melted butter or margarine
lemon slices

Drain oysters. Add cracker crumbs, salt, pepper, parsley, and 2 tablespoons melted butter; mix well. Place one halibut steak in a greased shallow baking dish. Sprinkle lemon juice over it and season to taste with salt and pepper. Spread the oyster stuffing over this and cover with the second steak. Fasten together with small skewers or toothpicks. Brush with melted butter. Bake in a 350 degree oven 40 minutes, basting frequently with more melted butter. Serve with slices of lemon. Serves 6.

PERCH WITH HOLLANDAISE SAUCE

2 pounds perch, red snapper, or other thick fillets
1 cup water
1 sliced onion
1 lemon slice
1 teaspoon salt
bay leaf
¼ pound bay shrimp
Hollandaise Sauce, see page 71

Thaw fillets if frozen and cut into individual portions. Combine water, onion, lemon, salt and bay leaf in skillet. Bring to boil. Cover and simmer 5 minutes. Add fish and simmer for 8 to 10 minutes until fish flakes easily when tested with fork. Rinse shrimp and drain well. Carefully remove fish to heat-proof platter and arrange ⅔ shrimp over fillets. Cover with foil and keep warm while preparing *Hollandaise Sauce*. Pour ½ of sauce over fish. Garnish with remaining shrimp and serve with remaining sauce. Makes 6 servings.

BAKED STUFFED POMPANO

1 pompano, about 2 pounds*
6 tablespoons butter or margarine
6-8 tablespoons white bread crumbs
2 tablespoons milk
2 egg yolks
1 tablespoon chopped tarragon
1 tablespoon chopped chives
salt and freshly ground pepper
⅔ cup white wine
3 tablespoons heavy cream
2 teaspoons chopped parsley

Preheat oven to 325 degrees. Without removing the head, carefully cut the fish along the backbone and remove the backbone. To make the stuffing, soften 4 tablespoons butter. Soak the bread crumbs in the milk and squeeze them dry; combine them with the butter, egg yolks, tarragon, chives and salt and pepper. Stuff the fish along the back where the bone has been taken out and carefully sew it up.

Put the fish in a very well-oiled baking dish, pour the wine over it, sprinkle with salt and pepper, dot with remaining butter and bake for 25-30 minutes. Transfer it carefully to a serving dish and keep it hot while you make the sauce. Bring the fish cooking juices to the boil and let them reduce to about half. Add the cream, parsley and a little salt, and boil until slightly thick and syrupy. Pour the sauce around and over the fish and serve at once. Makes 4 servings.

* Any non-oily fish may be substituted.

POMPANO AMANDINE

2 pounds pompano fillets
pepper
salt to taste
corn flake crumbs
½ cup slivered blanched almonds
butter or margarine

Season the fillets with pepper and salt if desired. Dip them into corn flake crumbs and place in a well-greased shallow baking dish. Sprinkle the fillets with the almonds and dot with butter. Broil, 3-inches from heat, until fish flakes easily with a fork (4 to 6 minutes). Be careful not to overcook. Serves 4.

RED SNAPPER PARMESAN

2 pounds red snapper or other fish fillets
1 cup sour cream
¼ cup grated Parmesan cheese
1 tablespoon lemon juice
1 tablespoon grated onion
½ teaspoon salt
dash Tabasco and paprika

Skin fillets and cut into serving size portions. Place in a single layer in a well-greased baking dish, 12X8X2-inches. Combine remaining ingredients except paprika. Spread sour cream mixture over fish. Sprinkle with paprika. Bake in 350 degree oven for 25 to 30 minutes or until fish flakes easily when tested with a fork. Serves 6.

SCALLOPED FISH

¼ cup butter or margarine
2 tablespoons finely chopped shallots or green onions
1 cup toasted bread crumbs
2 tablespoons flour
1¼ cups milk
1 pound cooked fish, flaked
1 tablespoon dry sherry
salt, pepper

Melt 2 tablespoons butter in saucepan over medium heat. Sauté shallots until tender. Stir in bread crumbs and toss. Remove and set aside.

Melt remaining 2 tablespoons butter in skillet. Stir in flour and cook 1-2 minutes until smooth. Slowly add milk and cook, stirring constantly, until thickened, about 3 minutes. Add fish and sherry. Season to taste with salt and pepper. Stir until blended.

Spread half fish mixture in buttered shallow baking dish and cover with half of bread crumbs. Top with remaining fish and bread crumbs. Bake at 425 degrees 20 minutes until sauce bubbles. Makes 4 servings.

COLD POACHED SALMON

1 (3-5 pound) whole salmon
4 cups water
2 cups dry white wine
1 large onion, sliced, with whole cloves stuck in it
2 stalks celery, sliced, with tops
2 carrots, sliced
1 tablespoon black peppercorns
½ lemon, sliced with peel
Dill Sauce

Cheese cloth can be used to wrap fish in with ends long enough to hang over edge of pot and then used as handles for lifting fish out of pan. Combine water, wine, onion, celery, carrots and peppercorns in fish poacher or roasting pan and bring to boil. Reduce heat, cover and simmer for 30 minutes. Lower fish into stock, cover and simmer over low heat for 20-35 minutes, about 7 minutes per pound. *Do not let stock boil.* When it is done, it can be flaked easily. Remove from heat and let cool in stock. When cool, remove from stock to serving platter and chill several hours. Prepare *Dill Sauce* and spread over fish or serve on the side. Can garnish with parsley and lemon slices. Makes 6 to 10 servings.

DILL SAUCE

1 cup sour cream
1½ tablespoons white vinegar
1½ tablespoons Dijon mustard
½ tablespoon brown sugar
2-3 tablespoons fresh dill, chopped

Mix all ingredients together and refrigerate several hours.

SALMON SAUTÉ WITH FRESH VEGETABLES

4 (4-6-ounce) salmon steaks
salt and pepper
¼ cup plus 2 tablespoons oil
¼ cup chopped green onions
¼ teaspoon thyme
1½ cups diagonally sliced zucchini or asparagus
1½ cups sliced mushrooms
¼ cup water
1 teaspoon grated lemon peel
lemon slices

Season salmon to taste with salt and pepper. Sauté in ¼ cup hot oil until browned on both sides. Allow 10 minutes cooking time per inch measured at its thickest part.

In separate skillet heat 2 tablespoons oil. Add green onions, ½ teaspoon salt and thyme and sauté 30 seconds. Stir in zucchini, mushrooms, water, and lemon peel. Simmer, covered, 2 minutes or until vegetables are crisp-tender. Remove to serving plate with slotted spoon. Garnish with lemon slices. Makes 4 servings.

SALMON DEVONSHIRE

1 (8-ounce) can stewed tomatoes, drained and chopped
¼ cup chopped onion
6 (6-ounce) salmon fillets
4 cups dry white wine
3 tablespoons butter
1 tablespoon cornstarch
½ pound mushrooms, chopped
1 small shallot, minced
½ cup whipping cream, whipped
salt and freshly ground pepper

Combine tomatoes and onion in small saucepan. Cover and simmer 30 minutes. Remove from heat and set aside. Poach salmon in wine until fish flakes with fork and has lost its translucency, about 10 minutes. Transfer to heatproof serving dish and keep warm. Increase heat to high and cook wine until reduced to about 1 cup. Transfer to small saucepan.

Combine 1 tablespoon butter and cornstarch to form paste. Place wine over medium heat and gradually whisk in paste. Cook briefly, whisking constantly until mixture thickens. Preheat broiler on high setting. Melt remaining butter in medium skillet. Add mushrooms and shallot and sauté about 3 minutes. Stir in tomato mixture. Spoon over salmon. Fold whipped cream into wine mixture. Season to taste with salt and pepper. Spread over fish and broil until golden brown, about 1-2 minutes.

BAKED SCALLOPS

1½ pounds scallops
flour
light cream
butter or margarine
salt and pepper

If any of the scallops are too large, cut them in half. Roll in flour and place in a greased pan so that each lays separately by itself - no layers. Pour in light cream to come just halfway up the depth of the scallops. Dot with butter and season with salt and pepper. Bake in a 350 degree oven 25 to 30 minutes. Serves 4.

SCALLOPS AND HERB SAUCE

1¼ pounds scallops, cut up if large
6 tablespoons white wine
1½ tablespoons butter or margarine
2 tablespoons chopped parsley
Sauce

Arrange scallops in oven-proof dish. Pour wine over and dot with butter. Sprinkle with parsley. Broil scallops about 4-inches from heat 3-4 minutes or just until they begin to brown. Do not overcook. Place scallops in serving dish, spooning some cooking liquid over. Serve sauce separately. Makes 4 servings.

SAUCE

½ cup chopped parsley
4 tablespoons minced shallot
3 teaspoons tarragon
1 teaspoon basil, minced
½ teaspoon white pepper
½ teaspoon chervil
2 cloves garlic, minced
½ cup white wine
2 tablespoons champagne vinegar
2 tablespoons lemon juice
¾-1 cup mayonnaise

Combine all ingredients but mayonnaise in blender container. Purée on high, then pour into small saucepan. Boil gently until reduced to ½ of its original volume. Strain liquid and return to pan. (Sauce can be prepared to this point several hours ahead, if desired). Stir in mayonnaise to blend and heat over low heat.

SCALLOP AND MUSHROOM PIE

15 large scallops (approximately 1¼ pounds)
½ pound white mushrooms, sliced
¾ pound potatoes
6 tablespoons margarine
salt and freshly ground pepper
1 heaping tablespoon flour
⅔ cup milk
milk and margarine for mashing
pinch of nutmeg
2-3 tablespoons heavy cream
bread crumbs

Preheat oven to 375 degrees. Wash scallops and pat dry. Peel and boil the potatoes. Meanwhile, melt 2 tablespoons margarine in a frying pan. Add the scallops, seasoned with salt and pepper, and sauté them for 2 minutes. In another pan, melt 2 tablespoons margarine and gently sauté the mushrooms for 5 minutes. Remove the mushrooms, add the flour to pan and make a sauce with the scallop juice and milk. Let the sauce cook while mashing the potatoes with milk and margarine. Stir the cream into the sauce; add the scallops and mushrooms. Put the mixture in a small pie dish; cover with mashed potatoes and sprinkle bread crumbs on top. Bake for 30 minutes or until lightly browned on top. Serves 3-4.

BAKED LAKE TROUT

1 (3-pound) trout
salt and white pepper
3 tablespoons melted butter
½ cup bread crumbs
2 teaspoons tarragon, finely chopped
2 teaspoons dill, finely chopped
2 teaspoons parsley, finely chopped

Split trout in half and remove bones and skin. Cut the
fish into serving portions and place in a greased baking
dish. Sprinkle with salt and pepper. Pour melted butter
over fish and sprinkle bread crumbs on top. Bake in a
350 degree oven for 30 minutes, or until fish flakes easily
with a fork. Baste occasionally. Ten minutes before fish
is to be done, sprinkle with herbs. Serves 4 to 6.

NEW ENGLAND SEAFOOD CASSEROLE

½ pound bay scallops
½ pound raw shrimp
½ pound crabmeat (imitation crabmeat may be
  substituted)
1 tablespoon butter or margarine
2 tablespoons onion, finely chopped
¼ cup dry sherry or vermouth
¼ cup clam juice
1 teaspoon salt
pinch pepper
juice of ¼ lemon
1 teaspoon paprika
1 teaspoon dry mustard
1½ teaspoons cornstarch in 2 tablespoons water
2 egg yolks
2 tablespoons cream (half-and-half may be substituted)
4 tablespoons mayonnaise

Wash seafood; shell shrimp. Dry all thoroughly. Melt
butter in frying pan and add scallops, shrimp, onion,
sherry, clam juice, salt, pepper and lemon juice. Stir in
paprika and mustard. Reduce heat to medium and cook
for 5 minutes. Remove scallops and shrimp to ovenproof
dish and add crabmeat. Add the cornstarch mixture and
continue cooking juices. Remove from heat. Beat yolks,
stir in cream and mayonnaise and fold into warm sauce.
Pour thickened sauce over seafood. Bake at 400 degrees
about 10 minutes or until golden brown. Serves 3-4.

FRIED CLAMS

1 egg, separated
½ cup milk
1 tablespoon melted butter
¼ teaspoon salt
½ cup flour, sifted
24 cherrystone or Ipswich clams, cleaned and drained

Beat egg yolk until thick and lemon-colored. Add milk and butter and blend thoroughly. Sift flour and salt together; add to egg mixture, and stir until smooth. Beat egg white until stiff and fold into egg yolk mixture. Dip each clam into the batter and fry in oil (375 degrees) until golden brown. Turn frequently to brown all sides. Drain on absorbent paper. Serves 4.

STEAMED CLAMS

Scrub the shells and carefully wash free of sand in several waters. Place in a large kettle with two cups of water. Cover and steam until shells open. Serve the clams while still very hot, with side dishes of melted butter and clam broth.

Allow 15 to 20 clams for each serving.

DEVILED CLAMS

1 tablespoon chopped onion
1 tablespoon chopped green pepper
1 tablespoon chopped celery
2 tablespoons butter
6 tablespoons flour
2 teaspoons dry mustard
Tabasco sauce to taste
½ teaspoon thyme
2 cans chopped clams, drained, reserving juice
2 cups clam liquor and milk
salt and white pepper
corn-flake crumbs

Sauté onions, green pepper, and celery in butter until soft but not brown. Add flour and dry mustard, and mix thoroughly into a stiff roux. Add Tabasco and thyme; mix well. Add clam juice mixed with enough milk to make 2 cups. Stir constantly until well blended and thick. Stir in clams, then add salt and white pepper to taste. Place the mixture in ramekins or baking shells. Sprinkle with corn-flake crumbs and dot lightly with extra butter. Bake in a 375 degree oven for 20 minutes or until nicely browned.

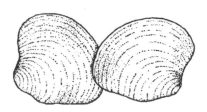

BROILED OYSTERS

12 oysters on half shell
rock salt
1 large mushroom, chopped fine
1 teaspoon minced onion
1 tablespoon butter
flour
½ cup warm milk
¼ cup cooked oatmeal
salt and pepper
1 tablespoon minced parsley
3 tablespoons grated Parmesan cheese
2 tablespoons melted butter

Sauté mushroom and onion in 1 tablespoon butter until soft, but not brown (about 10 minutes). Dredge with flour and stir to blend smoothly. Add milk and stir until thickened. Add oatmeal and stir well. Season to taste with salt and pepper; stir in parsley. Place oysters on rock salt (enough to hold them in place) on baking sheet. Place under 400 degree broiler heat for 4 minutes. Remove from broiler and cover each with sauce. Sprinkle each oyster with Parmesan cheese and a few drops of melted butter. Return to the broiler and cook until golden brown (about 5 minutes). Serves 2.

AVOCADO AND CRAB CASSEROLE

¼ cup diced green pepper
2 tablespoons minced onion
2 tablespoons minced celery
2 tablespoons butter or margarine
2 tablespoons flour
1 cup milk
½ cup sour cream
1 cup sharp cheddar cheese, shredded
½ teaspoon seasoning salt, such as *Old Original*
  Bookbinder's Crab and Shrimp Seasoning
½ teaspoon Worcestershire sauce
¾ to 1 pound flaked crab meat
1 ripe avocado, cut into crescents
1 tablespoon lemon juice
½ cup soft bread crumbs or ⅓ cup sliced almonds

Sauté green pepper, onion and celery in butter in saucepan. Blend in flour; add milk, then sour cream, stirring constantly. Cook over medium heat, stirring until thick and smooth. Add cheese, salt, and Worcestershire sauce; stir until cheese is melted. Fold in crab.

Turn into 1-quart baking dish. Sprinkle avocado crescents with lemon juice; arrange over top of crab mixture. Sprinkle with bread crumbs. Bake in preheated 375 degree oven 20 minutes until mixture is bubbly. Makes 4 servings.

CHESAPEAKE BAY CRAB CAKES

2-ounces butter or margarine
½ cup onion, finely chopped
½ cup celery, finely chopped
½ cup dry bread crumbs
1 egg, well beaten
2 teaspoons dry mustard
½ cup mayonnaise
1 tablespoon Worcestershire sauce
1 teaspoon paprika
⅛ teaspoon pepper
1 pound lump crabmeat, canned or fresh
½ cup oil

Sauté onion and celery in butter, but *do not brown.* Combine with all other ingredients. Fold in crabmeat, keeping the pieces as large as possible. Allow to chill. Form into cakes and fry in hot oil until browned on both sides. Makes 4-6 cakes.

Serving suggestion: Combine *Old Original Bookbinder's Crab Bisque Soup* with small amount of milk; heat, and spoon over crabcakes.

CRAB AND MUSHROOM SUPREME

½ pound fresh mushrooms
3 tablespoons butter
1 tablespoon lemon juice
¼ cup dry sherry
1 pint dairy sour cream
¾ pound fresh or frozen crab meat
3 tablespoons grated Parmesan cheese
4 English muffins
minced parsley

Slice mushrooms. Melt 1 tablespoon butter in large skillet. Add mushrooms and sprinkle with lemon juice. Sauté a few minutes, then add sherry. Let cook down until liquid is halved. Stir in sour cream. Add crab and cheese and heat through. Split and butter muffins, using remaining 2 tablespoons butter. Toast lightly under broiler. Arrange on serving platter and spoon crab sauce over muffins. Garnish with parsley. Makes 4 servings.

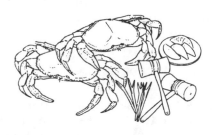

CRABMEAT AU GRATIN

1 pound lump crabmeat, fresh or canned
4 tablespoons butter
2 tablespoons flour
2 cups light cream
salt and pepper
½ cup seasoned bread crumbs
½ cup grated cheese

Melt butter and blend in flour, stirring until smooth. Add cream and cook over medium heat, stirring constantly, until thickened. Add crabmeat and continue cooking just long enough for the crabmeat to heat through. Season to taste with salt and pepper. Place in 4 ramekins. Mix bread crumbs and cheese and sprinkle over the tops. Dot with butter. Place under broiler and heat until golden brown.

CRABMEAT WITH PEPPERS AND MUSHROOMS

1 green pepper, thinly sliced
½ pound fresh mushrooms, sliced
4 tablespoons butter or margarine
1 teaspoon paprika
salt and pepper to taste
¾ pound crabmeat

Sauté peppers and mushrooms in 2 tablespoons butter just until tender. Remove from pan. Add remaining butter to pan and sauté crabmeat in skillet. When the crabmeat is hot, add vegetables, salt and pepper to taste. Serve with rice or on toast. Serves 4.

CRAB QUICHE

½ pound crab meat
1 (9-inch) pie shell
½ cup shredded Swiss cheese
⅓ cup minced onion
1 tablespoon minced parsley
1 tablespoon sherry
⅛ teaspoon leaf tarragon
3 eggs, slightly beaten
1 cup half-and-half
½ teaspoon salt

Flake crab. Bake pie shell in preheated 425-degree oven about 10 minutes but do not brown. Sprinkle cheese over bottom of partially baked pie shell. Toss crab lightly with onion, parsley, sherry and tarragon; arrange in layer over cheese.

With beater, blend eggs, half-and-half and salt just to mix; pour gradually over crab mixture. Bake in preheated 325 degree oven 45 to 50 minutes or until set. Let stand 5 minutes before cutting in wedges to serve. Makes 5 to 6 servings.

MARYLAND STYLE CRAB CAKES

¼ cup butter
½ cup flour
2 cups milk
1 egg, beaten
1 teaspoon salt
¼ teaspoon dry mustard
1 tablespoon Worcestershire sauce
2 tablespoons chopped fresh parsley
2 pounds lump crabmeat
Egg Batter, see page 71
bread crumbs
vegetable oil

Melt butter and blend in flour, stirring until smooth. Add milk and stir until thickened. Beat in the egg. Add salt, dry mustard, Worcestershire sauce and parsley and mix well; cool. Stir in crabmeat. Form into large cakes and chill thoroughly. Dip cakes in *Egg Batter*, then in crumbs, and fry in 375 degree oil until nicely browned (about 15 minutes). Serves 6.

SAUTÉED CRABMEAT

½ stick sweet butter
1 teaspoon paprika
1 pound lump crabmeat
salt and pepper

Melt butter in skillet. Add paprika and cook until brown. Add crabmeat, salt and pepper to taste. When the crabmeat is golden brown on one side, turn and brown other side. Can be served on slices of toast. Serves 3.

SEAFOOD CURRY

¼ cup olive oil
1 small onion, finely chopped
2 tablespoons flour
1 teaspoon curry powder
1 teaspoon salt
10½-ounce can cream of mushroom soup
3 cups combined lobster, shrimp, and crabmeat
¼ cup sherry
1 cup sour cream

Heat oil; add onion and brown lightly. Blend in flour, curry powder and salt. Stir until smooth. Add soup and cook over low heat until sauce comes to a boil. Mix in the sherry, seafood, and sour cream. Serve hot over rice or noodles. Serves 6.

BAKED IMPERIAL CRAB

¼ medium green pepper, diced
1 teaspoon diced pimiento
1 tablespoon butter or margarine
6 tablespoons mayonnaise
1 egg yolk
1¼ teaspoons seasoning such as *Old Original
Bookbinder's Crab & Shrimp Seasoning*
dash Tabasco sauce
1 teaspoon Worcestershire sauce
½ teaspoon dry mustard
1 pound fresh lump crabmeat
1 egg white, beaten stiff
lemon juice

Sauté green pepper and pimiento in butter just until tender. Place 5 tablespoons mayonnaise, egg yolk and 1 tablespoon seafood seasoning in mixing bowl. Add sautéed pepper mixture and mix thoroughly. Stir in crabmeat. Refrigerate for at least 30 minutes.

Preheat oven to 450 degrees. Spoon crabmeat mixture into 4 ramekins and bake for 10 minutes. Meanwhile beat egg white until stiff. Mix with remaining mayonnaise, lemon juice and remaining seafood seasoning. Remove ramekins from oven. Spread egg white topping over crabmeat mixture. Place under broiler for a few minutes until golden brown on top.

BAKED LOBSTER

4 (1-pound) lobsters
2 cups corn-flake crumbs
salt and pepper
¼ cup melted butter
¼ cup milk
¼ cup dry sherry
1 pound fresh crabmeat
melted butter

Split and clean lobsters (or have your fish dealer do this for you, but plan to cook them immediately). Remove stomachs and back veins, leaving all fat, tomalley, and juice.

Mix crumbs with salt, pepper, melted butter, milk, and dry sherry. Stir in crabmeat and mound mixture on top of lobsters. Pour melted butter over all. Bake in a 400 degree oven for 10-12 minutes. Serves 4.

BOILED LOBSTER

4 live lobsters
½ cup diced celery
1 onion, peeled
drawn butter, optional
lemon wedges

Place lobsters in a kettle of briskly boiling salted water to cover. Add celery and onion. Cover and bring back to boiling. Boil rapidly, covered, 6 to 8 minutes for 1½-pound lobsters. Remove from water, drain well, place each on its back and split down the body lengthwise. Remove stomach and intestinal vein. Serve with butter and lemon. Serves 4.

BROILED LOBSTER

1 live lobster
melted butter
paprika

Turn the lobster on its back and split from tail to head. Remove stomach, located at the head. Remove the long vein which runs the length of the lobster. Brush the flesh with melted butter and sprinkle with paprika. Place 6-inches from the broiler heat and broil as follows:

1 ¼ pound lobster	15 minutes
1 ½-3 pound lobster	25 minutes
3-4 pound lobster	30 minutes

LOBSTER NEWBURG

2 cups canned or fresh lobster*
2 tablespoons butter
salt to taste
cayenne pepper to taste
1 teaspoon paprika
4 egg yolks
1 cup light cream
½ cup dry sherry
1 tablespoon brandy, if desired

Melt butter in top of a double boiler over hot, not boiling water; add salt, cayenne pepper, and paprika. Beat egg yolks; add cream and sherry, and beat again to blend thoroughly. Slowly add egg yolk mixture to melted butter. Cook, stirring constantly, until thickened. Add lobster and continue cooking until lobster is heated through. Blend in brandy, if desired, and serve on toast or rice. Serves 4.

*Crabmeat or shrimp may be substituted.

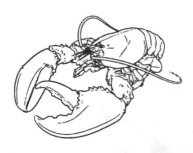

LOBSTER STEW

1 cup diced fresh lobster meat
3 tablespoons butter or margarine
1 clove garlic, finely mashed
¼ teaspoon Worcestershire sauce
dash Tabasco
4 cups scalded milk
2 teaspoons onion juice
½-1 cup clam broth
salt and pepper
paprika

Heat the butter and add the garlic, Worcestershire Tabasco, and lobster meat and sauté for 3-4 minutes. Slowly add the milk, onion juice and clam broth. Season to taste with salt, pepper and paprika.

LOBSTER THERMADOR

2 (2½-pound) lobsters
2 cups tomato sauce
½ cup tomato purée
2 tablespoons powdered chicken base
1 teaspoon Worcestershire sauce
1 bay leaf
2 cloves
2 whole allspice
¼ teaspoon nutmeg
1 veal bone
1 onion, chopped
3 stalks celery, chopped
salt and pepper to taste
3 tablespoons butter
2 tablespoons flour
1 tablespoon cornstarch
grated Parmesan cheese

Boil or steam lobsters. When cool enough to handle, split, remove meat, and dice it. Reserve the four half-shells. Place tomato sauce and all remaining ingredients except butter, flour, and cornstarch in a saucepan and simmer gently for an hour. Remove veal bone and bay leaf. Press remainder through a sieve or whirl in blender. Melt butter, add flour and cornstarch, and stir until smooth. Add a little of the tomato mixture and stir until smooth. Add to remainder of the tomato mixture and stir to blend well. Place lobster meat in sauce. Spoon into lobster shell halves, top with grated Parmesan cheese and broil, 3-inches from heat, 5 minutes or until golden. Serves 4.

PRAWNS AMARETTO

8 large uncooked prawns, cleaned
flour
2 tablespoons butter
2 tablespoons brandy
2 tablespoons amaretto
1 tablespoon dry white wine
2 teaspoons orange juice
¼ teaspoon grated orange peel
2 tablespoons whipping cream
2 teaspoons chopped parsley

Dredge prawns in flour. Melt butter in small skillet. Add prawns and sauté until browned on both sides. Remove from pan. Add brandy, amaretto, wine, orange juice and orange peel. Cook, stirring until liquid is shiny and slightly reduced. Add cream to sauce. Heat until sauce is slightly thickened. Add prawns. Sprinkle with parsley. Makes 2 servings.

SHRIMP AU GRATIN

2 cups chopped cooked shrimp*
¼ cup butter or margarine
¼ cup flour
2 cups light cream or half-and-half
1 cup grated cheddar cheese
salt and pepper
¼ cup bread crumbs

Melt butter; add flour and stir until smooth. Add light cream and cook over medium heat, stirring constantly, until thickened. Add half of the grated cheese and stir to blend thoroughly. Season to taste with salt and pepper. Stir in the shrimp. Place in one large casserole or in individual baking dishes. Cover with remaining grated cheese, mixed with bread crumbs. Dot with butter if desired. Bake in a 400 degree oven 20 to 25 minutes, or until delicately browned. Serves 4.

*Other cooked and flaked fish may be substituted for shrimp.

SHRIMP IN MUSTARD SAUCE

20-25 extra large shrimp, shelled and deveined
salt
freshly ground pepper
4 tablespoons safflower oil
2 medium shallots, minced
2 tablespoons minced fresh tarragon
½ cup dry sherry
½ cup whipping cream
½ cup unsalted butter or margarine,
  cut into small pieces
2 tablespoons Dijon mustard
1 tablespoon minced chives

Season shrimp with salt and pepper to taste. Heat oil in large pan until oil begins to smoke. Add shrimp and sauté over high heat 6-7 minutes. Transfer shrimp to warm plate and keep warm. To pan, add minced shallots and 1 tablespoon minced tarragon. Sauté 2-3 minutes. Add sherry and cream and reduce sauce until thick enough to coat spoon. Whisk in butter, one piece at a time. Just before serving, whisk in mustard, but do not let sauce boil as mustard will become grainy. Adjust seasonings.

Arrange shrimp on serving plate and pour sauce over shrimp and sprinkle with chives. Serves 3-4.

RICE AND SHRIMP SUPREME

1 tablespoon unsalted butter or margarine
2 tablespoons flour
1½ cups half-and-half
½ teaspoon dill weed
½ teaspoon paprika
⅛ teaspoon Tabasco sauce
1 pound peeled, deveined shrimp
½ cup sliced green onion, with tops
¼ cup diced pimiento
3 tablespoons grated Parmesan cheese
3 cups hot cooked rice*

Melt butter in 3-quart saucepan. Stir in flour. Add half-and-half, dill, paprika and Tabasco. Cook, stirring, over medium heat until thickened and bubbly. Add shrimp and cook until shrimp turns pink, 3 to 5 minutes. Stir in onions, pimiento and cheese. Heat through. Serve over rice. Serves 3-4.

*Note: ⅛ teaspoon Tabasco sauce may be substituted for salt when cooking rice.

FRIED SHRIMP

½ cup flour
¼ teaspoon salt
1 egg, slightly beaten
⅛ cup milk
2 dozen shrimp, shelled and cleaned
Egg Batter, see page 71
lemon wedges
Tartar Sauce, see page 72

Sift together flour and salt. Add egg and milk and beat until smooth. Dip shrimp into *egg batter* and fry in deep hot (365 degrees) oil until golden brown. Turn while frying to brown all sides. Serve with lemon wedges and *tartar sauce* if desired. Serves 4.

SHRIMP SCAMPI

3 pounds jumbo, uncooked shrimp,
  shelled and deveined
½ cup olive oil
salt and pepper
8 cloves garlic, finely chopped
½ cup finely chopped parsley

Sauté shrimp in hot oil for 5 minutes. Remove to hot serving platter and season with salt and pepper. Add chopped garlic and parsley to oil remaining in the pan and cook for 1 minute. Pour this sauce over the shrimp and serve immediately. Serves 6.

SHRIMP BOATS

¼ cup dry bread crumbs
¼ cup butter or margarine
¼ cup chopped onion
1 pound shrimp, shelled and deveined
2 tablespoons spicy prepared mustard
½ teaspoon salt
⅛ teaspoon tarragon
pepper
¼ cup dry white wine
2 avocados, halved and peeled

Toss bread crumbs with 2 tablespoons melted butter and set aside. Sauté onion in 2 tablespoons butter until transparent but not browned. Add shrimp and cook until pink. Stir in mustard, salt, tarragon, pepper to taste and white wine. Remove from heat. Arrange avocado halves in shallow oven-proof serving dish. Spoon shrimp and sauce into shells. Sprinkle 1 tablespoon buttered bread crumbs over each avocado half. Slide under broiler and broil 3-inches from heat until lightly browned, about 1 minute. Garnish with watercress if desired. Makes 4 servings.

SHRIMP CREOLE

1 pound peeled tomatoes
½ cup diced celery
¼ cup diced green pepper
¼ cup minced onion
3 tablespoons butter or margarine
¾ pound uncooked shrimp, peeled and deveined
1 teaspoon sugar
½ teaspoon salt
⅛ teaspoon pepper
1 bay leaf
1 small sprig parsley
¼ teaspoon Worcestershire sauce
1⅓ cups Minute Rice

Drain tomatoes measuring liquid; add water to liquid to make 1⅓ cups. Sauté celery, green pepper and onion in butter until lightly browned. Add shrimp and cook until shrimp turns pink. Add measured liquid, the tomatoes, sugar, salt, pepper, bay leaf, parsley, and Worcestershire sauce. Cover and simmer 3 minutes. Stir in Minute Rice (right from box). Cover and simmer an additional 5 minutes. Remove bay leaf and parsley before serving. Makes 3-4 servings.

SHRIMP DU JOUR

3 pounds uncooked shrimp, shelled and deveined
1 cube butter or margarine
2 teaspoons Worcestershire sauce
2 cloves garlic, chopped
¼ cup chopped chives
¼ cup chopped parsley
salt and pepper
grated cheese
bread crumbs
drawn butter, optional

Sauté shrimp in butter with Worcestershire sauce, garlic, chives, parsley, salt, and pepper for 5 minutes. Reserve the liquid and place mixture in a large casserole and sprinkle with grated cheese and bread crumbs. Pour liquid over all and bake in a hot (400 degrees) oven for about 8 to 10 minutes or until golden brown. Serve with drawn butter. Serves 6.

SPICY SKEWERED SHRIMP

24 extra large shrimp
Spicy Marinade, see page 74

Shell and devein shrimp. Place in marinade, turning to coat all sides. Marinate at least 30 minutes. Thread 3 shrimp onto each of 8 bamboo skewers that have been soaked in water. Grill 2-3 minutes per side.

STIR-FRIED SHRIMP WITH
TOMATOES AND FRESH BASIL*

1¾ pounds extra large uncooked shrimp, peeled and
deveined
2 tablespoons olive oil
1 red onion, cut into ⅛-inch dice
1 (28-ounce) can chunky pasta-style stewed tomatoes
4 tablespoons balsamic vinegar
salt
red pepper flakes to taste
⅔ cup julienned fresh basil leaves
grated imported Parmesan cheese

Heat 1 tablespoon oil in wok or heavy non-stick skillet
over high heat. When very hot, add shrimp and cook until
pink and just done. Remove from skillet. Add another 1
tablespoon olive oil and chopped onion. Stir-fry until
heated through, about 2 minutes.

Add tomatoes with liquid, balsamic vinegar, salt and red
pepper flakes to taste. Boil 2 minutes. Add shrimp. Stir-
fry 30 seconds until hot. Adjust seasonings to taste.
Add basil leaves. Toss well. Serve hot with grated
Parmesan cheese. Makes 4 servings.

*Cheese ravioli may be substituted for shrimp: use 1-2
(9-ounce) packages of fresh ravioli.

SWORDFISH MIRABEAU

1½-2 pounds swordfish, cut into 1-inch thick steaks
fresh ground pepper
oil
anchovy paste
anchovy fillets
green olives, sliced
chopped parsley

Wash and dry swordfish steaks, and sprinkle both sides with pepper. Put the steaks on broiling rack and brush the top with oil flavored with anchovy paste to taste. Broil the steak about 2-inches from heat for 6 to 7 minutes. Turn steaks over, brush the uncooked side with anchovy paste and broil for 4 minutes longer. Transfer the swordfish to a serving dish and keep warm while assembling the garnish.

Cover the top with a latticework of anchovy fillets and fill the spaces in between with slices of green olives. Surround the steaks with a border of finely chopped parsley. Serves 4.

SWORDFISH WITH PEPPERS AND OLIVES

swordfish steak (1 per serving)
vinegar and oil dressing (2 parts vinegar to 1 part oil)
1-2 shallots, diced
pitted Greek olives, rinsed (5-6 per steak)
chopped marjoram or oregano to taste
olive oil
salt and pepper to taste
red bell pepper, roasted, peeled and cut into strips

Season swordfish with salt, pepper, and 1 teaspoon of olive oil per steak. Combine all other ingredients including olives and peppers, as if making a salad dressing. Grill, broil, or barbecue swordfish. Spoon dressing over steaks, arranging olives and peppers attractively. Dressing may be heated if necessary.

BROILED SWORDFISH SUSANNAH

4 tablespoons butter or margarine
½ cup minced onion
½ cup minced carrot
½ cup minced fennel or celery
¼-⅛ cup peeled, seeded and chopped lemon
1½ tablespoons capers, rinsed and drained
salt and freshly ground pepper to taste
2 (8-ounce) swordfish steaks, 1-inch thick
salt and white pepper
1 lemon, thinly sliced
2 tablespoons butter or margarine
½ cup dry white wine
fresh dill for garnish

Preheat oven to 350 degrees. Melt butter in large skillet over medium heat. Add onion and sauté until just transparent. *Do not brown.* Increase heat to medium-high; add carrot, celery, and lemon and sauté until mixture is thick and glazed, about 10-12 minutes. Add capers and sauté an additional minute. Season with salt and pepper. Turn into a shallow baking dish, spreading evenly to cover bottom.

Rinse fish and pat dry. Arrange in single layer atop vegetables. Sprinkle with salt and white pepper. Place lemon slices over steaks and top each steak with 1 tablespoon butter. Pour wine over the fish and vegetables. Cover dish tightly with foil and bake 20 minutes. Remove foil and bake an additional 5 to 10 minutes, or until fish flakes when touched lightly with fork. Transfer fish and vegetables to warm serving platter and garnish with fresh dill. Serves 2.

Desserts

APPLE WALNUT PIE

6 large apples, sliced
1½ cups sour cream
1 egg
1 cup granulated sugar
2 teaspoons vanilla
¼ cup flour
pinch of salt
Pie Shell
Topping

Mix ingredients together, fill the unbaked pie shell and bake in a preheated 450 degree oven for 10 minutes, then at 350 degrees for 30-40 minutes. Stir filling.

Place topping on top of pie filling. Bake for 15 minutes at 350 degrees.

PIE SHELL

1¾ cups flour
¼ cup granulated sugar
1 teaspoon cinnamon
½ cup cold butter

Combine ingredients, roll out crust and place in a 10-inch pie pan.

TOPPING

⅓ cup brown sugar
⅓ cup granulated sugar
½ cup flour
1½ teaspoons cinnamon
pinch salt

½ cup cold butter
1 cup chopped walnuts

Combine flour, sugars, cinnamon and salt in bowl. Cut in butter until crumbly. Stir in walnuts.

PEANUT BUTTER PIE

1⅛ cups graham cracker crumbs
⅓ cup sugar
1 stick unsalted butter, melted
12-ounces cream cheese, room temperature
1½ cups peanut butter, smooth
1½ cups sugar
2 cups whipping cream, whipped, reserving 1 cup for top
powdered sugar

Preheat oven to 350 degrees. To prepare crust, combine graham cracker crumbs, sugar, and melted butter in a mixing bowl and stir together thoroughly. Press the mixture into the bottom and sides of a 9-inch pie tin. Bake for 8 minutes and set aside to cool completely.

Mix the cream cheese, peanut butter, and sugar together in a large bowl until well blended. Fold in one cup whipped cream; spoon the filling into the cooled crust. Whip remaining cup of whipping cream with powdered sugar to taste until stiff. Spoon over pie and refrigerate for at least 4 hours. Makes 8 portions.

PECAN PIE

2 eggs
½ cup sugar
1 tablespoon flour
⅓ cup butter, softened
1 teaspoon vanilla
1 cup light caro syrup
1 cup chopped pecans plus some extra for top of pie

Beat eggs. Beat in sugar, flour and butter. Add vanilla, caro syrup and 1 cup pecans and blend. Pour into unbaked 8 or 9-inch pie shell. Bake in preheated 400 degree oven for 15 minutes. Reduce to 325 degrees for 35-40 minutes.

PIE CRUST

1 teaspoon salt
2 cups sifted flour
⅔ cup shortening
¼ to ⅓ cup ice water

Combine salt and flour. Cut in shortening. Slowly add ice water. Put in refrigerator for one hour before baking. Makes 2 (9-inch) crusts.

MELBA STREUSEL PIE

1 (10-ounce) package frozen sliced peaches,
  fresh peaches may be used
1 (10-ounce) package frozen raspberries, drained
¼ cup sugar
3 tablespoons corn starch
¼ teaspoon cinnamon
1 teaspoon lemon juice
Pecan Crust, see page 190
Topping

Prepare crust. Thaw frozen fruit and drain. Sprinkle
lemon juice over fruit. Combine sugar, corn starch, and
cinnamon. Add to fruit mixture, mix well and turn into
pastry lined pan. Bake in a preheated 375 degree oven
30-35 minutes until center of filling is partially set.
Sprinkle with streusel topping and bake 10-15 minutes
more until golden brown. If top gets too brown, cover
with aluminum foil.

TOPPING

2-ounces butter
¾ cup flour
½ cup brown sugar

Combine ingredients until crumbly.

RASPBERRY CHEESE PIE

1 pound cream cheese, softened
⅔ cup sugar
3 eggs
1¼ teaspoons vanilla
unbaked graham cracker *Pie Crust*, see page 190
Glaze

Preheat oven to 325 degrees. Beat the cream cheese in mixer until smooth. Gradually beat in the sugar and then the eggs, one at a time. When the mixture is very smooth, blend in the vanilla. Pour the mixture into the pie shell and bake until set, about 40 minutes. Remove from the oven and chill for at least 2 hours before topping with *Glaze*.

GLAZE

1½ teaspoons unflavored gelatin
5 tablespoons cold water
3½-4 cups raspberries
½ cup sugar
dash nutmeg

Mix the gelatin and 2 tablespoons cold water. Set aside to soften the gelatin. Mash 1½ cups of the raspberries slightly, with a fork, and place in a small saucepan with the remaining 3 tablespoons of water. Simmer over low heat until very soft. Remove from the heat and press through a sieve, reserving the juice. Discard the seeds and pulp. Return the juice to the saucepan and add the sugar, gelatin mixture, and nutmeg. Cook over low heat until the gelatin and sugar are dissolved.

Chill until thickened but not firm, stirring occasionally. Gently stir the remaining raspberries into the glaze.

Spoon the coated raspberries over the pie. If desired, the remaining glaze can be poured over pie. Chill until firm.

FRESH COCONUT CUSTARD PIE

4 eggs, well beaten
½ cup sugar
¼ teaspoon salt
2 cups hot milk
½ teaspoon vanilla
1 cup freshly grated coconut
1 (9-inch) unbaked pie shell

Combine the beaten eggs, sugar, and salt; add milk very gradually, stirring constantly so that the custard does not curdle. Stir in the vanilla. Spread the coconut over the bottom of the unbaked pie shell and pour custard mixture over it. Bake in a preheated 450 degree oven 10 minutes; reduce heat to 350 degrees, and bake 25 to 30 minutes longer, or until a knife inserted in the custard comes out clean.

AMARETTO CHOCOLATE CAKE

4 (1-ounce) squares unsweetened chocolate
½ cup butter or margarine
⅞ cup hot water
2 cups sifted cake flour
2 cups sugar
¼ teaspoon salt
1 cup sour cream
1 teaspoon vanilla
1½ teaspoons baking soda
2 eggs, beaten
1 cup semisweet chocolate pieces
6 tablespoons amaretto liqueur
1 teaspoon almond extract
1½ cups whipped cream
1 cup sliced strawberries
Chocolate Glaze
¼ cup chopped almonds

Melt unsweetened chocolate in top of double boiler over hot water. Combine butter and hot water in small saucepan. Bring to boil. Stir in melted chocolate.

Resift flour with sugar and salt. Pour chocolate mixture into flour mixture all at once. Blend well. Mix in sour cream, vanilla and baking soda. Stir in beaten eggs to blend. Fold in semisweet chocolate pieces, 2 tablespoons amaretto and almond extract. Turn into 2 greased 9-inch layer cake pans. Bake at 350 degrees 30 minutes or until cake is done. Spoon remaining 4 tablespoons amaretto on cake layers. Cover and let stand to cool.

Combine 1 cup whipped cream with sliced strawberries. Fill between cake layers and frost with *Chocolate Glaze*. Garnish top border with remaining ½ cup whipped cream.

Sprinkle center with chopped almonds and garnish with more strawberries, if desired. Makes 8 to 12 servings.

CHOCOLATE GLAZE

4-ounces semisweet chocolate, chopped
6 tablespoons (¾ stick) sweet butter or margarine
2 tablespoons light corn syrup
1 teaspoon water

Melt chocolate and butter in a small saucepan. Remove from heat and stir in corn syrup and water. If too thin, let sit until it thickens slightly. Pour warm glaze over top of cake, allowing it to drip down the sides.

BANANA CAKE

1 ½ cups sugar
½ cup vegetable shortening
2 eggs
3 cups flour
1 ½ teaspoons baking powder
1 ¼ teaspoons baking soda
¼ teaspoon salt
3 very ripe bananas, mashed
1 teaspoon vanilla
1 cup sour cream

Cream sugar and shortening together; add eggs and mix again. Stir in mashed bananas and vanilla.

In a bowl, combine flour, baking powder, baking soda and salt. Add this to banana mixture, alternating with sour cream. Pour into 2 greased and floured 10-inch round pans or 3 (8-inch) round pans. Bake in a preheated 350 degree oven for 35 to 45 minutes.

14-CARROT CAKE

2 cups flour
2 teaspoons baking powder
1½ teaspoons baking soda
1 teaspoon salt
2 teaspoons cinnamon
2 cups sugar
1½ cups oil
4 eggs
2 cups grated carrots
1 (8½-ounce) can crushed pineapple, drained
½ cup chopped nuts
Cream Cheese Frosting

Preheat oven to 350 degrees. Sift together dry ingredients: flour, powder, soda, cinnamon, and salt. Add sugar, oil, eggs and mix well. Stir in carrots, pineapple, and nuts. Put in three (9" layer) cake pans or one 13X9 pan. Bake for 35 to 40 minutes.

CREAM CHEESE FROSTING

½ cube margarine or butter
1 (8-ounce) package cream cheese, softened
1 teaspoon vanilla
2 cups sifted powdered sugar

Combine butter, cheese, and vanilla. Beat until well blended. Add sugar gradually, beating vigorously. If it is too thick, add a small amount of milk.

COCONUT CAKE

4 eggs, separated
½ cup oil
½ cup water
1 teaspoon vanilla
½ teaspoon salt
1½ teaspoons baking powder
1 cup cake flour
¾ cup plus 3 tablespoons sugar
Custard Filling
1½ cups whipping cream
3 cups freshly grated coconut

Mix egg yolks, oil, water and ½ teaspoon vanilla. Add salt, baking powder, cake flour and ¾ cup sugar. Mix until smooth. Beat egg whites until stiff and fold into batter. Pour into 10-inch springform pan that has been greased and floured or lined with wax paper. Bake in a preheated 325 degree oven 50 minutes or until cake tests done. Cool.

Cut cake into 3 or 4 layers. Spread cooled *Custard Filling* between cake layers. Whip cream with 3 tablespoons sugar until stiff. Frost top and sides of cake with whipped cream. Sprinkle top and sides generously with coconut.

CUSTARD FILLING

2 cups milk
¾ cup sugar
½ teaspoon vanilla
1 tablespoon cornstarch
2 tablespoons cold milk
2 eggs, beaten

Combine milk, sugar and vanilla in saucepan. Bring to boil. Mix cornstarch with cold milk and beaten eggs; blend this into sugar mixture and cook, stirring, until thickened. Cool.

CARNIVAL CAKE

2 cups flour
1 cup dark brown sugar (packed)
½ cup granulated sugar
3 teaspoons baking powder
1 teaspoon salt
½ teaspoon soda
½ cup shortening
1¼ cups milk
3 eggs
1½ teaspoons vanilla
1 cup semisweet chocolate pieces (6-ounces)

Heat oven to 350 degrees. Grease and flour two (8 or 9-inch) round layer cake pans or a bundt pan. Measure all ingredients into large mixing bowl. Blend ½ minute on low speed, scraping bowl constantly. Beat 3 minutes on medium speed, scraping bowl occasionally. Pour into prepared pans. Bake 40 to 45 minutes or until toothpick inserted in center comes out clean.

LEMON GLAZE CAKE

1 (1-pound 2¼-ounce) package yellow cake mix
1 (3½-ounce) package instant lemon pudding mix
4 eggs
¾ cup oil
¾ cup water
Lemon Icing

Combine yellow cake and lemon pudding mix with eggs, oil and water. Mix well 2 to 3 minutes with mixer. Turn into ungreased (12-cup) bundt pan and bake in preheated 350 degree oven 40 to 50 minutes or until cake springs back when lightly touched. (Cover with foil if cake is getting too brown). Remove from oven.

While warm, pierce surface of cake with tines of fork and pour *Lemon Icing* evenly over cake. Makes 10 to 12 servings.

LEMON ICING

½ (1-pound) box powdered sugar, sifted
⅓ cup lemon juice
1 tablespoon melted butter or margarine
1 tablespoon water

Combine powdered sugar, lemon juice, melted butter and water and beat with mixer until smooth. Pour over cake while still warm.

Variation: Use orange pudding mix in place of lemon pudding mix and orange icing instead of lemon icing, using orange juice in place of lemon juice.

CHOCOLATE ALMOND COFFEECAKE

2 cups granulated sugar
4 eggs, beaten
½ cup butter or margarine
4 cups sifted flour
1 tablespoon baking powder
1 teaspoon baking soda
2 cups sour cream
½ cup chocolate almond liqueur
¾ cup brown sugar, packed
½ cup chopped pecans
½ cup chopped walnuts
½ teaspoon cinnamon

In large mixing bowl, beat granulated sugar, eggs and butter until well blended. Sift together flour, baking powder and soda. Fold dry ingredients into creamed mixture.

Stir in sour cream and liqueur. Place half of batter in greased and floured 10-inch tube pan. Set aside.

In small bowl, combine brown sugar, pecans, walnuts and cinnamon. Sprinkle half of nut mixture on top of batter in pan and swirl lightly. Cover with remaining batter, then sprinkle with remaining nut mixture; swirl lightly. Bake in a preheated 375 degree oven 1 hour and 15 minutes.

POPPY SEED CAKE

1 cup poppy seeds
⅓ cup honey
¼ cup water
¾ cup butter
¾ cup sugar
1 tablespoon grated lemon zest
2 teaspoons vanilla
2 eggs
1 cup sour cream
1 teaspoon salt
2½ tablespoons lemon juice
2¼ cups flour
1 teaspoon baking soda
½ teaspoon baking powder
Lemon Glaze

Butter and flour 1 (10-inch) angel food tube pan. Set aside. Preheat oven to 325 degrees.

Combine poppy seeds, honey and water in saucepan and cook over low heat 5-7 minutes or until water evaporates, stirring frequently. Cool.

Cream together butter, sugar, lemon zest and vanilla. Add eggs, 1 at a time, beating well after each addition. Add and combine thoroughly at low speed sour cream, poppy seed mixture, salt and lemon juice. Sift together flour, baking soda and baking powder. Add flour mixture to poppy seed mixture. Beat at low speed until thoroughly combined. Pour batter into prepared pan. Bake at 325 degrees about 60 to 75 minutes or until cake draws from sides of pan and center is dry when tested. Cover with foil if cake browns too quickly. Cool about 15 minutes in pan. Invert and cool to lukewarm. Pour hot *Lemon Glaze* over cooled cake. Makes 1 (10-inch) cake.

LEMON GLAZE

6 tablespoons lemon juice
¾ cup powdered sugar

Combine lemon juice and powdered sugar in saucepan. Bring to boil and boil 1 to 2 minutes or until thin syrup is formed.

MOIST APPLE CAKE

6 apples, diced
1 cup raisins
½ cup nuts
2 cups sugar
3 cups flour
2 teaspoons baking soda
½ teaspoon cinnamon
½ teaspoon salt
2 eggs
1 cup oil
1 teaspoon vanilla

Preheat oven to 350 degrees. Combine apples, raisins, nuts, and sugar. In a large bowl, mix together flour, soda, cinnamon, salt, eggs, oil and vanilla. Blend in the apple mixture. Pour into a greased bundt pan. Bake for 60 minutes.

CRUNCHY APPLE AND RAISIN TART

¼ pound dark raisins
4 golden delicious apples
½ cup unsalted butter
ground cinnamon
¼ cup granulated sugar
filo dough
melted butter
powdered sugar
4 sprigs mint

Place raisins in saucepan with water to cover and bring to boil. Remove from heat and set aside.

Peel and core apples. Cut each into 10 segments, then sauté in butter until tender. Drain raisins. Add to apples along with 1 tablespoon cinnamon and granulated sugar.

Stack 3 sheets filo, each brushed with melted butter, on top of each other. Cut sheets into 5-inch squares. Place 1 stacked filo square, buttered side up, in oven-proof skillet brushed well with melted butter. Top with ¼ apple mixture, then second filo square. Sprinkle top with powdered sugar and bake at 400 degrees 5 to 6 minutes or until golden brown.

Remove skillet from oven and heat over burner until filo is browned on bottom. Invert onto serving plate. Sprinkle top with additional powdered sugar and cinnamon and garnish with mint sprig. Repeat procedure to make 4 servings.

SACHER TORTE

1 cup butter
1 cup sugar
12 eggs, separated
8-ounces semi-sweet chocolate
2 cups cake flour
Apricot Glaze
Chocolate Glaze, see page 171

Beat butter and sugar until light and creamy. Beat in 10 egg yolks, 3 at a time. Add chocolate, melted and cooled, and mix well. Fold 12 stiffly beaten egg whites into the batter and sift in flour as the egg whites are folded in. Bake the cake in a greased and floured spring-form pan in preheated 350 degree oven until it tests done. Remove the rim and let the cake rest for 24 hours. Cut the cake horizontally into 3 layers. Spread *Apricot Glaze* over two of the layers and ice the entire cake with chocolate icing. Serve with sweetened whipped cream.

APRICOT GLAZE

Heat apricot jam over hot water, thin it with a little water, and flavor it, if desired, with a little apricot brandy to taste.

BROWN PEAR BETTY

4 cups sliced fresh pears
¼ cup orange juice
¼ cup white sugar
½ cup brown sugar, packed
¾ cup flour
dash salt
½ teaspoon cinnamon
¼ teaspoon nutmeg
½ cup butter or margarine

Place pears in a buttered 9-inch pie plate and drizzle with orange juice. Combine sugars, flour, salt, cinnamon and nutmeg. Cut in butter until mixture is crumbly and sprinkle over pears. Bake at 375 degrees 40 minutes or until the topping is crisp and golden. Serve warm with cream or whipped cream. Makes 6 servings.

RICE PUDDING

1 cup converted rice
6 cups milk
pinch salt
¼ teaspoon nutmeg
1½ teaspoons vanilla
⅓ teaspoon cinnamon or ¾ cinnamon stick
¾ cup sugar
2 tablespoons melted butter

Rinse rice in water and drain. In saucepan, mix together milk, salt, nutmeg, and cinnamon. Add rice and bring to boil. Immediately lower heat and simmer for one hour, stirring occasionally. Stir in sugar, vanilla, and butter. Continue on simmer for 30-45 minutes longer. Pour into a baking dish and brown lightly under the broiler. Allow to cool. Chill thoroughly before serving.

OUTRAGEOUS CHOCOLATE MOUSSE

Nabisco Famous Chocolate Wafers (22)
3 tablespoons melted butter
12-ounce package chocolate chips
4 eggs, separated
3 teaspoons dry instant coffee (if using freeze-dried,
   melt in water)
3 teaspoons rum
2 cups whipping cream

Preheat oven to 350 degrees. Crush cookies in blender. Mix with melted butter and press into bottom of spring-form pan. Bake in oven for 8 minutes.

Melt the chocolate chips over hot water and cool; add coffee and beaten egg yolks. Beat egg whites until stiff and add to mixture along with rum. Whip cream and add to mixture. Pour into pan and refrigerate overnight.

CHOCOLATE SWIRL CHEESECAKE

1 cup semisweet chocolate pieces
sugar
1¼ cups graham cracker crumbs
¼ cup butter, melted
2 (8-ounce) packages cream cheese, softened
½ cup sour cream
1 teaspoon vanilla
4 eggs

Combine chocolate pieces and ½ cup sugar over hot (not boiling) water. Heat until chips melt and mixture is smooth. Remove from heat and set aside.

Combine graham cracker crumbs, 2 tablespoons sugar and melted butter in a small bowl, mixing well. Pat into 9-inch springform pan, covering bottom and a little up the side. Set aside.

Beat cream cheese in large bowl until light and creamy. Gradually beat in ⅓ cup sugar. Mix in sour cream and vanilla. Add eggs, one at a time, beating well after each addition. Divide batter in half. Stir melted chocolate mixture into one portion and pour into crumb-lined pan. Cover with plain batter. With a knife, swirl plain batter with chocolate batter to marbleize. Bake in preheated 325 degree oven for 50 minutes or until almost solid in center. Cool at room temperature and refrigerate until ready to serve.

CHEESECAKE

18 graham crackers, ground fine
¼ cup sweet butter, melted
1 tablespoon sugar
24-ounces cream cheese, softened
1 cup sugar
4 eggs
1½ teaspoons vanilla
Topping

Combine graham cracker crumbs, butter and 1 tablespoon sugar and press into bottom of 9 or 10-inch spring-form pan.

In electric mixer, mix together cream cheese, 1 cup sugar, eggs, and vanilla for 20 minutes. Pour over crust and bake in a preheated 375 degree oven for 30 minutes. Turn off oven, open door and leave cake inside for 1 hour. Take cake out of oven and preheat oven to 475 degrees. Mix topping ingredients together, spoon over top of cake and put back in oven for 7 minutes. Let cool, cover and refrigerate for at least 24 hours.

TOPPING

1 pint sour cream
1½ teaspoons vanilla
3 tablespoons sugar

CLASSIC BURNT CREAM DESSERT

1 pint whipping cream
4 egg yolks
½ cup sugar
1 tablespoon vanilla
Sugar Topping

Heat whipping cream over low heat until it bubbles around edge of pan.

Beat egg yolks and sugar until thick, about 3 minutes. Gradually beat cream into egg yolks. Stir in vanilla and pour into 6 (6-ounce) custard cups. Place custard cups in baking pan with about ½-inch water in bottom. Bake at 350 degrees 20 to 25 minutes. Remove from water and refrigerate until chilled. Sprinkle each custard with about 2 teaspoons Sugar Topping. Place on top rack under broiler and cook until topping is bubbly and brown, but not scorched. Chill before serving. Makes 6 servings.

SUGAR TOPPING

¼ cup granulated sugar
1 teaspoon brown sugar

Combine sugars and mix well.

STRAWBERRY MOUSSE

2 boxes strawberries, hulled and puréed
4 eggs, separated
1½ cups sugar
1 cup heavy cream, whipped
1 envelope unflavored gelatin
1 teaspoon vanilla (liqueur can be used)

Beat egg whites until stiff. Soften gelatin in ¼ cup water and beat until melted. Beat yolks and sugar until thick and lemony.

Stir in strawberries and melted and cooled gelatin mixture. Fold in whipped cream and beaten egg whites. Refrigerate.

FROSTY LIME SOUFFLÉ

5-7 limes
6 eggs, separated
1 ¼ cups sugar
2 envelopes unflavored gelatin
¼ teaspoon salt
1 ½ cups hot water
1 cup whipping cream, whipped

Juice enough limes to measure ½ to ⅔ cup juice. Slice 1 lime thinly and set aside. Beat egg yolks lightly. Stir in ¾ cup sugar, gelatin, salt and lime juice. Gradually add hot water. Cook and stir 5 minutes or until gelatin is dissolved. Chill, uncovered, about 45 minutes or until mixture mounds, stirring occasionally.

Beat egg whites until foamy. Gradually add remaining ½ cup sugar and beat until stiff peaks form. Fold gelatin mixture into beaten whites. Fold in whipped cream. Fit 6-cup soufflé dish with foil collar. Spoon ⅓ cup soufflé mixture into dish arranging a few lime slices around edge of dish. Add remaining mixture and remaining lime slices. Chill at least 4 hours. Before serving, remove foil collar. Makes 10-12 servings.

GRAHAM CRACKER CRUST

graham crackers (20 halves)
¼ cup sugar
5 tablespoons melted butter or margarine
¼ teaspoon cinnamon

Finely crush graham crackers. Blend all ingredients well in a mixing bowl. Put in a 9 or 10-inch springform pan or 9-inch deep-dish pie pan and press firmly to form crust.

PECAN CRUST

3 tablespoons granulated sugar
1½ tablespoons light-brown sugar
¾ cup flour
6 tablespoons unsalted butter, melted
1½ teaspoons vanilla
¾ cup finely chopped pecans

Combine sugars, flour, melted butter, vanilla and pecans. Mix well, then evenly pat onto bottom of 9-inch springform pan.

INDEX